EAT, DRINK
& SUCCEED

Kirsten!

Cheers.

EAT, DRINK & SUCCEED

Climb Your Way to the Top Using
The Networking Power of Social Events

LAURA SCHWARTZ

BLACK OX PRESS

NORTH AMERICA

Published by
Black Ox Press
North America
www.blackoxpress.com

Edited by Amy Carr
Copyedited by Mike Burke
Cover Design by Carrmichael
Author Photograph by John Reilly
Interior Design by Zach Dodson

First Edition
10 9 8 7 6 5 4 3 2 1

Library of Congress Control Number: 2010900356

ISBN: 0-615-34453-4
ISBN 13: 978-0-615-34453-9

Set in Book Antiqua | Printed in the United States of America

To Mom, Dad and Andréa, who encourage me to
climb at every rung of my life's ladder.
Thank you for being my guides and safety net below.

TABLE OF CONTENTS

ACKNOWLEDGEMENTS

My most important title doesn't have "The White House" in front of it or even a seal that goes with it, as nothing makes me prouder than to be a daughter and sister. Whether being called "Denny and Judy's daughter" or "Andréa's sister," I am so blessed. Mom, Dad and Andrea, you have all taught me how to climb to my goals with perseverance, respect and gratitude by bringing me along on your ladders, sharing your bridges and teaching me how to build mine. I am forever thankful.

I also gained an entire family in my publisher, the Black Ox Press. To my editor Amy Carr, you have taken my voice and put it to paper as only a seasoned writer, mentor and friend could do. I respect you for your professional talents and personable approach. You asked questions, challenged my answers and made me a better person and this, a better book. Thanks to my copy editor Mike Burke, who took every comma, space and word seriously. To Carrmichael Design -- Michael, you're talented and tough. I learned from you and about myself along the way. Thanks to your team, Lucia Keller and Jason Hendricks. To Zach Dodson, thank you for your time and talents as they are reflected throughout the pages. And to Carson and Zach, thanks for your parents. You guys are an awesome reflection of them both.

To President and Secretary Clinton: I would never have been 19 growing up in the White House ranks without your support. You looked past my age and instead at my attitude, work and results. You taught me more than I could have ever learned from a textbook, including it's not just what you're saying, it's why you are saying it that counts, and that conversation isn't something you just have – it's something you invest in. I learned about helping others, to believe in myself and the world. And in that same respect, you showed me the world. Thank you.

To the White House Staff, working alongside you was both a personal and professional life-changing experience. Most especially to the volunteers, you adopted me into all your families and, with inspired dedication, each did the work of two staff members. To the White House Ushers Office, Residence Staff and Operations guys – you truly are the backbone of history and always had my back. I love you all!

To Larry King, whether on air or in commercial break our conversations were fun and sitting across from you, priceless.

To Sir David Frost, the BBC, Oxford University, Al Hurra and GMTV UK: You allow a girl from Wisconsin to speak with the world and I treasure all of your accents. Thank you.

Thanks to Fox News Channel, it's line-up and my producers – you always pushed me to be prepared and I'm stronger for it.

To Joe Scarborough, having you introduce me with that game-day announcer's voice is always exciting!

To the *CBS Early Show*, thanks for the "Trail Mix," and the opportunity to transition from policy, strategy and percentages to actual people, passion and pop culture.

To my wonderful family and friends! From Chicago to Ireland, Australia and beyond, thank you for your support and for being such an important part of my life.

To the reader! Thanks for giving this book, which I have thought about everyday since January 2001, a place on your coffee table, office or bathroom. Wherever this is, I'm, thrilled!

INTRODUCTION

OPRAH WINFREY DID IT.

Steven Spielberg did it.

Laura Schwartz from small-town Plymouth, Wis., did it.

And now it's time for you to do it, too.

I may not have much in common with the world's most powerful television host and an Academy Award-winning movie mogul, but all three of us have found life-changing opportunity in unlikely places. Oprah mapped out her future on a napkin while on a date at Hamburger Hamlet. Spielberg cooked up the idea for DreamWorks while socializing at a White House state dinner. And I went from answering phones to producing the President on the world stage everyday.

We all knew that as social and ordinary as any situation appears, it's business. And by the time you finish this book, you, too, will be able to unleash "The Networking Power of Social Events." It's a lesson I was fortunate enough to learn on one of the most high-profile stages in the world—the White House in Washington, D.C.

My transition from a volunteer who answered phones to the point person behind more than 1,000 White House events, including 12 state dinners and the nation's Millennial celebration, was made possible by my ability to harness my social power. My story may be unique, but my ability to turn conversation into opportunity is not. One thing I've learned from my fabulous friends, colleagues and mentors all over the world is each one of us is powerful and we're all social. The secret is knowing when, where and how to use that power to reach your goals or to help someone else reach theirs.

While watching, listening and being a part of conversations and deals that took place behind the scenes at White House events over eight years, I discovered the fine line between business and pleasure has long been erased. A state dinner at the White House, aside from the fact that it's black-tie and the most coveted party invitation in the political power scene, is nothing more than a business meeting disguised in Versace and Armani. At these events, major deals were clinched even before the President and visiting head of state asked everyone to raise their glasses for the first ceremonial toast.

One of the most notable examples of this occurred at the Sept. 29, 1994, state dinner for then Russian President Boris Yeltsin. Three guests – Steven Spielberg, David Geffen and Jeffery Katzenberg – who had been invited separately, found themselves talking through dinner and late into the night about their common interests. Thirteen days later, they announced one of the biggest partnerships and film studios of all time, DreamWorks. Spielberg recalled the night in his 1999 biography *Steven Spielberg: A Biography by Joseph McBride*: "We're in tuxedos talking about a brand new studio and just across from us there's Yeltsin and Bill Clinton talking about disarming the world of nuclear weapons."

But you don't have to be at a state dinner to make a powerful networking connection.

For Oprah, the most important change of her career came about as the result of some doodles on a napkin at a Hamburger Hamlet restaurant. Those doodles came from none other than Pulitzer Prize-winning film critic Roger Ebert, who took Oprah to the hamburger joint on a date years ago when she was hosting *AM Chicago* and contemplating syndication. She had offers from both ABC and King World, but was leery of syndicating her show, as Ebert recounted in a 2005 article in the *Chicago Sun-Times*. Ebert, who knew plenty about syndication thanks to his popular show *Siskel & Ebert at the Movies,* had little trouble convincing her syndication would be more lucrative and the way to go. He wrote:

> "I took a napkin and a ballpoint pen, and made some simple calculations.
>
> *Line 1: How much I made in a year for doing a syndicated television show.*
>
> *Line 2: Times 2, because Siskel made the same.*
>
> *Line 3: Times 2, because Oprah would be on for an hour, instead of half an hour.*
>
> *Line 4: Times 5, because she would be on five days a week.*
>
> *Line 5: Times 2, because her ratings would be at least twice as big as "Siskel & Ebert."*
>
> ...I pushed the napkin across the table."

And the rest is history…

It's time to start looking at social obligations as career opportunities. A cocktail party could be a place to just eat and drink, or it could be your chance to Eat, Drink and Succeed! I'm not suggesting you slip your resume under someone's drink at an event, but do use your napkin as your "to-do" list, your master plan! Turn the long line to the open bar into a one-on-one "chance" meeting. You can easily open with your passion for the evening's cause and close by arranging your next meeting in someone's corner office. But take note: those three minutes in line may be the only time you get to make an impression. You're going to have to make every second count. That's why it's crucial to start exercising your networking power before you even pick up your ticket.

Your ability to pull off a networking power play in under three minutes rests on various powers that you need to practice, plan and rehearse. Whether it's a business lunch, annual conference, birthday party or black-tie gala, you have the power to make every event beneficial and the power to make yourself remembered.

Over the pages ahead we'll look at all these opportunities and learn how to make the most of them. I want you to use this book as a reference point, textbook and a checklist for your next event. The Networking Power of Social Events is your key to getting ahead. The next time you head out to an event, you'll be ready to get more out of it than just the free food and drink. You'll be ready to climb while you Eat, Drink AND Succeed!

HITTING MY MARK

"IT'S SHOWTIME."

When all of the prep work for a White House event was done, after I briefed the President and he was ready to take center stage, I would turn to him one last time and ask "OK sir, ready?"

"Yes, Sarge," he typically replied. "We call her Sarge," he'd often explain to everyone in the room. "Everybody wants to tell me what to do, and she gets to do it everyday."

As I cue the conductor of "The President's Own" United States Marine Band to begin "Hail to the Chief," a sense of calm would come over me as the President would look my way and utter those two words I heard before almost every event: "It's Showtime."

Just like a live theater performance, every bill signing, press conference, military ceremony or state dinner involved countless hours of preparation, practice and perfect timing before the "show" itself. It was my job to make sure it all went off without a hitch, but no one knew better than President Clinton that when the moment arrived, it was up to him to be focused, communicate his message, make an impression and get the job done.

Saying those two words was his way of getting in the proper mindset, putting everything else aside and concentrating on the immediate task ahead. It's such a powerful, lasting thought that when I was given the opportunity to engrave a message on a brick in the walkway leading up to the Clinton Library, I immediately knew what it should say: "It's Showtime. Laura Schwartz."

Since then I've incorporated that sentiment into my daily life. Whenever I am walking into an important meeting, black tie gala, happy hour, keynote or luncheon, I just whisper to myself, "It's Showtime," and everything comes into focus.

It's just one of the many lessons I learned in the White House, and one of the tips I hope you'll take away from my story and experiences. This book is about you and how you can find opportunity at every turn. To help you understand how these techniques can truly work, let me tell you how I turned social power into the opportunity of a lifetime.

◆ CLIMBING THE HILL ◆

I was fingerprinted at the White House in January of 1993 - not for crashing a party or jumping the fence, but as part of my FBI security check as a 19-year-old volunteer in the press office. I was spending the second semester of my sophomore year in the Washington Semester program at the American University. I thought it would be a fun experience. As you'll see, it wasn't just fun, it was forever life-changing.

As a part of the program, students were free to spend two days a week volunteering or interning in the District. One of my first days at AU, my roommate mentioned that a guy who participated in the program a few years earlier had called her journalism professor to say that he was on President-Elect Clinton's transition team and would be serving in the White House Press Office. He was reaching out for volunteers because the White House Intern Program was not yet in place and he knew they would need help. I called him, met with him the next day and was getting my fingerprints taken a few days later. He warned me that he had no idea what awaited anyone as they were just coming from a campaign and into the White House. Most likely I'd be answering phones, making copies, which was cool with me because I was doing those mundane tasks...at The White House!

The pace was fast to say the least. I sat at a desk alongside wonderful volunteers, most of them retired, and some former campaign staff waiting to be placed in Administration positions. We answered the phones from morning till night. I was in the Office of Media Affairs, part of the Press Office, which housed the four regional press secretaries, the Director of Television, Director of Radio, and the Director of Specialty Press.

I answered calls from people whose names I'd never heard before: Mack McLarty (Chief of Staff and Clinton's trusted friend since kindergarten), Maggie Williams (First Lady's Chief of Staff and close friend), Bruce Lindsay (counsel to the president and his confidant since the '60s). I took down their names and messages, and would figure out what events and issues were imminent, but had no idea how events got on the President's schedule or how the office executed media coverage.

If I was going to learn, I had to teach myself. To familiarize myself with the White House staff, I started keeping detailed notes on a pad of paper I kept next to the phone about the people who called the office. Then, when the "Transitional Phonebook for the Executive Office of the President" came out, I "borrowed" a copy. I would read it on the Metro to and from the office to memorize the names and titles. For the first time in my life, I started reading the daily newspaper so I could see if any of these people were quoted and to understand what was going on without asking so many questions.

Whenever a staff member needed copies made or press releases faxed, I was happy to volunteer. I didn't care that it meant getting toner on my hands; it was an opportunity to see what was going on. I'd always make an extra copy of everything for myself and place it in a folder that sort of became my self-made textbook for the press office. I always kept it with me and it became my greatest resource.

By taking phone messages, I could figure out what events were happening and which staff members were the most involved with the events of the day. Then I would approach the staff member in charge, mention that I didn't have class on the day of their event (even though I usually did) and offer to help out if they needed an extra hand. What can *I* do for *you* became my mantra.

Soon I began escorting media crews from the gate to the Rose Garden. Now, instead of sitting in a classroom or on the phones, I was standing in the press area watching the President give a speech. Afterward, I escorted crews back to the gate and then headed back to the office to see if there was anything else needed. The staff members started to know my name as I was always up for helping out, staying late or coming in early. The volunteers got in around 8:30 a.m. and stayed until about 7 p.m.

I was the early bird arriving by 7 a.m. and staying until some of the last staff from the office walked out around 10 p.m.

Before long, a regional press secretary asked if I had ever written a press release. I confidently answered "Yes!" though I had never written one in my life. I took an old press release out of my folder and added the new information I was given into the existing format and...just like that, my first press release was edited and approved!

From there, I began writing more releases, escorting media crews that interviewed the President as well as the television crew that videotaped messages and executed live satellite media tours with the President. This gave me a great opportunity to watch, learn and ask questions while we were waiting for the President to arrive. (Note: There was a lot of waiting time – we called it CST "Clinton Standard Time," which was...late).

My semester ended in April but I felt like my adventure was just beginning. There was so much left for me to learn. I was still on the phones at times, but more often working one-on-one with the staff and learning more than I could in any college course. I talked to my parents and sister; they all agreed staying and learning was better than any paid job back home for the summer.

A few months later, the one paid receptionist in the office was leaving and the director of the office, Jeff Eller, offered me her position. I respectfully declined, saying I'd rather remain an unpaid volunteer being able to work with media and staff at events than be relegated back to the phones. Eller made me a deal and turned the paid slot into a position as a staff assistant. I would still have to manage the office and make sure the phones were covered, but I could continue working with staff and I got paid. I was thrilled, and so was my family! I turned 20 and had a job in the White House. Though at first I tried to fit in college through correspondence courses, I rarely opened a book until after midnight and ultimately decided to drop the classes and focus on my firsthand experience at the White House.

◆ WHEN OPPORTUNITY STRIKES, ◆ BE READY!

Everywhere I looked, there were new opportunities, and I was determined to take advantage of them. In September of 1993, the push for universal health care got under way and I was sent on the road to staff some of the First Lady's television interviews while the Director of Television traveled with the President. This was a big responsibility, but thanks to all the interviews I'd watched from the back of the room, I knew what to do and stepped right in!

Then one day we received a media request from a college newspaper, a call that typically would be handed to the specialty press secretary. I asked her if I could help out with college media (since I was that age and felt tuned in to their issues) and was told I could handle all college calls!

A few weeks later after a national press conference in the East Room, I had an idea for a college press conference. Instead of the national press in the chairs in the East Room – I would fill it with college reporters and then have the national media in the back of the room covering it as an event. The President could open with a brief statement and take questions from the college students – just like a national press conference. It would give the students an amazing experience and the President an opportunity to address questions about education, health care and jobs in relation to students and young adults. I submitted a formal proposal, the Press Secretary and Chief of Staff signed off on it and it was added to the schedule! The event was a great success and I was so proud to have taken the idea to fruition.

In 1994, the Midwest Press Secretary left, and I, along with the other press secretaries, helped fill in. Then something incredible happened: I was offered the job. I had done a good job filling in, but only because I had prepared myself from the earliest days as a volunteer with that pad of paper next to my phone, by making copies, reading the paper and adopting the attitude of "What can I do for you?"

As Midwest Press Secretary, I spent my time reaching out to reporters, fielding their questions and traveling five days ahead of the President whenever he traveled to the Midwest. I also still filled in for the Director of Television whenever he was double-booked. I loved television. I grew up in a family photography business and to this day I am still most comfortable when I'm in a studio filled with cameras and lights. Eventually, the Director of Television got an opportunity to go to work for MTV and in October of 1995, I was asked to take his position.

Wow. I never would have dreamed I would be offered that job. I never thought that job would ever be open! Yet there I was, always ready to help out and when the opportunity presented itself, I was ready to jump in! Now, instead of traveling ahead of the President, I was traveling with him aboard Air Force One when he did interviews on the road. I produced all of his satellite teleconferences, media tours, videotapings and live satellite events at the White House. I learned how to do all of these things through firsthand experience by seeing everything as an opportunity, paying attention, asking relevant questions (at the right times) and always being available to lend a hand.

When the '96 campaign came around I was able to take time off and hop aboard the President's campaign train, "The 21st Century Express," from Huntington, W.V., to Chicago for the Democratic National Convention. Being on that train and and being part of history was one of the best experiences of my life. I coordinated television interviews and the satellite into the convention, all the work I'd typically do at the White House... on a moving train! Best of all, I was right in the thick of things like coordinating affiliate television coverage of the President's victory speech from the Statehouse in Little Rock, Ark., when President Clinton was re-elected on Nov. 5, 1996.

In October of 1997, again something happened I never could have imagined in my wildest dreams. Sarah Farnsworth, the White House Director of Events since 1993, left the position and the Clintons asked me to come over to the East Wing as the new Director of Events. I was just floored! I so respected that position. Sarah handled it with grace, always right there with the President and First Lady, heads of state, cabinet secretaries, members of Congress, astronauts, celebrities – everyone and anyone who participated in various programs, visited or played a role at the White House.

Overnight, I found myself building on what I learned in the role as Director of Television to create events on what we referred to as the "18 acres" of the White House. It was better than having a front seat to history...I had a behind-the-scenes role in history.

I, Laura Schwartz from Plymouth, Wis., was now responsible for producing bill signings, Presidential press conferences, State Arrival Ceremonies and Dinners, America's Millennium Celebration, NATO's 50th Anniversary and even a White House Carnival. It was the busiest, most stressful and incredible time in my life! I tried to "zoom out" whenever I could to take it all in.

There was so much to learn, but the 12 state dinners I coordinated offered the most valuable White House lesson. It was here I realized that an event – even one as glamorous and high-profile as a state dinner – is really a networking opportunity in black tie!

It became clear to me that as social as any event may appear, it is business. But I also learned the event is only as powerful as the guest makes it. I watched plenty of guests, including politicians, celebrities and even foreign delegations, squander the opportunity to make powerful connections and instead leave events with nothing more than a stash of White House hand towels in their pockets. But I also saw what I now call "the Networking Power of Social Events" unfold on a grand scale as business partnerships were forged while music played and champagne flowed.

My White House experiences exceeded my wildest expectations, but when the Clinton Administration ended, I was determined to build on the lessons I learned and the relationships I developed in eight years in Washington. After leaving the White House, I continued to work with President Clinton, traveling around the world for the Clinton Foundation and the President's lecture series. Instead of just touching down in a country, doing a speech and getting back on the plane, there was time to explore, speak with and learn from the people in countries such as war-torn Bosnia, emerging Ghana, historic Slovenia and beautiful Norway.

In late spring 2004 when Sen. John Kerry was the inevitable nominee for the Democratic Party, I was asked to join the campaign as Teresa Heinz Kerry's Trip Director. During the Clinton/Gore '96 re-election campaign, I was only on the road for the big events; this time I was out 24/7 traveling with the senator and Teresa, meeting people in every corner of the country and learning more about life in America than any history book could ever teach.

When we lost the election I called up a Fox News Channel producer I knew through the late-night parties with the traveling press. I reminded her that I had been to the '93 Inauguration as a bright-eyed college student and played a behind the scenes role in '96 at the Capitol and even sat on the dais for the swearing in as well as walked in the parade with the press pool behind the Clintons as they walked from the Capitol to the White House. And in 2000, I was at the Vice President's Residence on the night of Gore's concession speech. I could speak to what was happening behind the scenes from all sides in a way few others could.

A few days later, I appeared on Fox News to give color commentary about the Inauguration. They brought me back for the State of the Union address and then signed me as an on-air political analyst. I was soon on air four to five nights or early mornings a week. From the *O'Reilly Factor* to Saturday morning's *Cavuto on Business*, I was a regular and was making connections that continue to help me today.

Though I had been happy to provide the Democratic perspective on Fox News, by the fall of 2007, I wanted to express a more independent voice and began providing political analysis on message, communications and strategy on *Larry King Live* for the primaries. At the start of the general election, I moved to the *CBS Early Show* to talk about the lighter side of politics in a segment we created called "Trail Mix." At the same time I started going international, giving an American perspective on world events and politics with Sir David Frost on *Frost Over the World*, the BBC and Britain's GMTV throughout the UK.

My achievements exceeded my wildest expectations, but I never forgot that I got there by finding networking opportunities, big and small, in everyday experiences. I've been teaching others how to do the same thing since two weeks after the Clinton Administration ended in January 2001, when I began giving public speeches about the Networking Power of Social Events. It's a concept I believe in so passionately I've decided to devote my first book to it. This is the culmination of everything I've learned from my days growing up in Plymouth, Wis., to my years at the White House and beyond.

The types of partnerships I've nurtured to build a career and a life can play out every day in your world, too, at annual conferences, cocktail parties, client dinners, political fundraisers and even Little League games. But first, you've got to realize your career isn't 9 to 5, it's 24/7, and as social as any event may appear, it's business. In the pages of this book, I'll give you specific tools to help you unleash your networking power. Get ready ladies and gentlemen…it's SHOWTIME!

THE POWER OF NETWORKING

NETWORKING CAN HAVE such a manipulative connotation. In fact, I even debated whether to use the word because it can sometimes suggests a motive like "What can you do for me?" or "What can I get from you?" As if the only reason to create a relationship is to get something. I don't subscribe to that negative definition and prefer to ask, "What can I do *for* you?" I really believe it's in helping others achieve that we achieve ourselves.

One of the most popular political speeches of all time mirrors my approach to networking. It's found in President John F. Kennedy's famous 1961 Inauguration speech: "Ask Not What Your Country Can Do For You; Ask What You Can Do For Your Country." And that's just it! Ask not what others can do for you; ask what you can do for others. Because by asking and doing for others, you'll start to realize what you can do for each other.

I figured this out at a very young age growing up in our family photography business in Plymouth, Wis. Through my parents and their business, I learned it's the relationships you build, respect and trust that become the source of your information, resources, clients and partnerships – and ultimately the basis for your success. If you ask anyone in Plymouth for words that describe my parents, you'll probably hear "positive," "genuine" and "helpful." That's how they have approached their network.

Photography was just a hobby for my dad when I was very young, until he lost his full-time job as traffic manager for A&P Cheese to a company merger. Now he and my mom, who had left her head nursing job to stay home with me and my sister, Andréa, had to decide what to do next. With their combined business savvy, my dad's talent and their savings, they started a photography studio.

They were entering a scary new world, and knew they'd need clients. Little did they know, they'd been building up a client base for years without even trying.

My dad had been taking pictures of family and friends for years. They even took a group shot of our class every year for fun and gave copies to our classmates at St. John Lutheran School. My parents were also active in the church and school. From hosting coffee hour after church, brunches with friends and their kids, sitting on the school board, leading the Parent Teacher Association, serving on church boards and organizing the school and church Christmas parties and summer picnics, my parents were always anywhere there was a party, need or cause. They would show up early to set up, while my sister and I would play with the other kids. They had their wine and Old Fashioned cocktails and we had our soda and Kool-Aid. My parents were naturally social, and, of course, my sister and I were, too!

Through all of those events and their involvement, my parents knew just about everyone including the teachers and administrators of the school, our classmates and their parents. They were the first to volunteer if the school needed to raise money or find chaperones for a field trip. Now, after being involved for more than eight years in the school and 15 in the church, they had ready-made clients to start the business. There were family pictures to take, weddings to schedule and senior pictures to line up.

Through the years, the business expanded to include undergraduate student pictures. They met with principals throughout the county and soon went from taking photos of 25 kids in my class to snapping shots of more than 6,000 students a year.

Their involvement in school, church and service and professional organizations like the American Legion, Lions and the local chamber of commerce turned out to be the smartest business moves they could have made, and an important early lesson for me.

I watched my parents network – not from a manipulative approach, but in a positive, genuine way that built long-lasting relationships and partnerships that later fueled their success.

I may have grown up in a small town (Plymouth, population 6,023), but I moved to Washington, D.C. (population 632,323), am now based in Chicago (population 3 million) and I've been fortunate to travel the world (population 7 billion). No matter what the size, geography, demographics, cultures or socioeconomic backgrounds in neighborhoods, cities, states and countries, I've found that face-to-face partnerships still produce the best results.

My parents were using the Networking Power of Social Events without ever realizing it. Now it's time to put it to work for you. It's all about face-to-face communication in new and unique places that will give you a competitive edge in the workplace. It's time to look at networking in a different and improved capacity, asking not just "Where do we want to go?" but "How are we going to get there?"

♦ BUILDING BRIDGES ♦

I often liken networking to building a bridge, as in: "What resources, whether people or product, do I have that can be your bridge to get to where you are going?" Maybe I think in terms of "bridges" because I've always liked how exciting it is to cross them, whether suspended over water, a deep ravine, small creek or a canopy bridge over the rain forest. I can't wait to see what's waiting on the other side. Or maybe it's because of my time on the Clinton/Gore 1996 campaign trail, when we were "Building a Bridge to the 21st Century." Some days building that bridge wasn't easy. We couldn't do it alone. We needed the majority of the electorate to pitch in, vote and help us achieve our goals. As exciting as crossing that next bridge may be, I've learned I can't cross, or even find it, without the help of others. I know, too, that sometimes I'll be called on to help others build their own bridges – bridges that I may very well have to cross myself someday.

It's a concept worth adding to our evolving definition of networking: **Networking:** *What Can I Do For You? Building bridges for others that someday we may want to cross as well. An attitude that is positive, genuine and helpful.*

After giving my seminars around the world on this very definition of networking, I asked myself what else can I do for college graduates, aspiring entrepreneurs, established CEOs, nonprofit organizations and anyone who wants to expand and improve themselves professionally? Then I realized it: Detail the Networking Power of Social Events on paper for others to see. So, even if you get only one thing from this book, take it from this page and every time a sales associate or bartender asks: "What can I do for you?" Repeat it to someone else later in the day. You'll feel better knowing you're paying it forward, and you'll be building a bridge that might even help you down the road.

Now that I've defined **what** I believe networking is, let's look at some overlooked places **where** we can use it. Then, of course, we'll get to the **how** to use it and **keep it going!**

SETTING THE SCENE

JUST AS A PLAY OR MOVIE uses many different scenes to advance the plot, your life is filled with "social scenes" that can take your story to the next level. Whether it's your buddies from the gym, parents from a Little League game, work colleagues or fellow volunteers, the people who make up your social scenes represent untapped opportunity. It's time to learn how, with a slight change of focus, you can turn the power within your untapped social scenes today into professional success tomorrow.

The Line Between Business and Pleasure Has Been Erased

We've all been asked as we leave for a trip: "Are you going for business or pleasure?" We're even prompted to check a box for "business" or "pleasure" when we make an airline reservation. I don't accept the premise of that question or the simple choice of one or the other because there is no either/or answer. What there should be is a box that says "both."

I believe the line between business and pleasure has long been erased! Realize that, and you'll find your social scenes are filled with career growth opportunities.

Just as my parents built a successful business through their social network, you can reach your goals by tapping into your own social connections. No goal is too small or too big. Whether you want to land an incredible job, increase your client base, get a promotion or start your own business, you can reach any and all of your goals just by looking at your "social" life in another way.

As Social as any Function May Appear, It Is Business

The sooner you realize that there is more to any "social event" than meets the eye, the sooner you will realize the opportunities for professional and personal growth at everyday social events. Attending a charity fundraiser can lead to a new career; an office birthday party may be the key to a promotion; a baseball game may produce a new client; and a dinner at a conference can produce a game-changing partnership.

Your Job May Be 9 to 5. Your Career is 24/7.

We have seen the evolution of the "work day" and it's longer than ever, especially now that smart phones keep you tethered to your colleagues and clients whether at your desk or on vacation. We try to still cling to that mental notion of "9 to 5" as a way to keep us sane. In reality, we'd be better off realizing our careers are 24/7 and that, through our activities and actions, we are non-stop "ambassadors" of what and whom we represent. There is no "on the clock"/"off the clock" approach to life anymore. Every time we head out to play golf, go to happy hour, attend a gala or drop in on friends, we punch in on the virtual clock.

Punching In on the Virtual Clock

Sometimes it seems we can't escape the ticking clock. Whether it's a deadline or biological, there are days we can't get that *Jeopardy* jingle out of our head. But for our purposes, the virtual clock isn't about counting down to the last second, it's about making every second count. This clock is a way of understanding that we can "punch in" at a bar and recruit new clients or develop fresh business ideas that will increase our value in the office. In fact, we can be just as effective, if not more, as when we are actually sitting at our desks! When you start walking into social events with a time card in your head, your goals will be achieved and you'll get more out of the event than just a few free drinks.

Effectively Tap Into Your Social Scenes

In four easy steps, you can tap into your current and future social scenes to reach your goals:

1. Recognize your current social scenes.
2. Look for new opportunities to expand your social and professional reach.
3. Start to actively build bridges for others to meet their goals.

4. Identify the people and bridges that could help you achieve your goals.

Recognizing our Social Scenes

Social scenes come in all different shapes and sizes. They may be big or small, professional or non-professional. Yet as different as some scenes may appear, they all share one common denominator: they all have the potential to be powerful.

Each one of us belongs to many different social scenes. Some we belong to by default and others we immerse ourselves in to seek results. They do not have to be large or well known or even traditionally labeled, because when two people are gathered anywhere, anytime, in any atmosphere, great things can happen. That's why you must find the power in your current social scenes, learn to tap into others and realize the power within them all.

Social Diagramming: Finding Your Power

What are your social scenes? Some of us may have a good grasp of our social connections, but even the most seasoned networker can overlook opportunities right in her own backyard. To find your current social scenes, I created an exercise I call "Social Diagramming."

I've always been a visual person. If I can see where I am on a map, I can figure out a way to get where I am going. That's exactly how I look at "Social Diagramming." I am able to see where I am and create a map to get to where I want to be professionally and personally. By diagramming your scenes, you'll find out where the hidden potential lies. By keeping it handy and revising it not just once but a few times a year, you will see how it grows whenever you change professions, have another child, get a new neighbor or become involved in another project. So, grab a large sheet of paper and a pencil – because your scenes are never written in stone and are constantly growing.

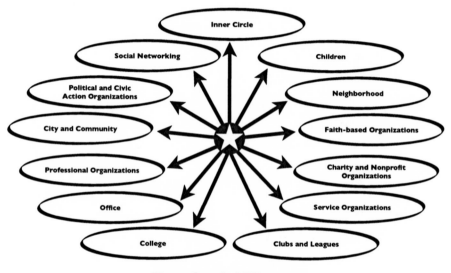

Your Social Diagram

I start every diagram with a giant star – like the "You are here" icon on a mall map. From your star, you are able to see where your bridges exist and where other bridges can be built both for yourself and those you meet.

While you do this, keep in mind, I'm all about building bridges for others: bridges that will benefit you, as well. In the quest to connect "A" to "C", you've got to have a "B". Be the "B"! Build a bridge and unlock the power to help someone change his or her life.

Let's get started on your diagram. We all run in different circles of friends, organizations and events that make up our social scenes, but we all base them around ourselves, which is why everyone starts with the big star – and that's you.

To help you get started, I've identified the "Lucky 13" most common social scenes. Some may not apply to you, or you may have additional scenes of your own to add.

1. Inner Circle
2. Children
3. Neighborhood
4. Faith-based Organizations
5. Service Organizations
6. Charity and Nonprofit Organizations
7. Clubs and Leagues
8. College
9. Office
10. Professional Organizations
11. City and Community
12. Political Organizations and Civic Action Groups
13. Social Networking

◆ INNER CIRCLE ◆

Everyone has an Inner Circle. It can be made up of your closest family, spouse, significant others, friends, colleagues, partners – the people you rely on and support day in and day out. If you and someone in your Inner Circle sat side by side to create your social diagrams, chances are you'd identify a number of common bridges and those that could benefit you both. For me, the Inner Circle begins with family.

My Inner Circle Bridge

Almost all of my social scenes in Chicago have been developed through bridges my sister, Andréa, built for me. I moved to the city in 2001 and she literally took me in. She had already been living in Chicago for 10 years when I came back from Washington. (That's 10 years of a social diagram that she had on her side.) Today, I've built off of hers, and she, mine. And because we share so many of our bridges, if I can't help someone to get to where they want to go – I can most certainly tap into the power of Andréa's social scene to get it done!

My first post-White House speaking engagement came through Andréa's connections. Andréa had known Chicago socialite Sugar Rautbord for five years and shared many stories with her about visiting me at the White House. In 2000 Sugar was in charge of building a speaker list for the Miss USA Pre-Pageant Convention, called "Women Power," in Gary, Ind., the site of that year's pageant. Sugar put me in contact with the convention and they asked me to speak on how beautiful White House state dinners are. I agreed on the condition I could mix some substance in with the fluff. My core message became: "As social as any event may appear, it is business. But the power of the event lies in the hands of the guests, and I know we are all social and all powerful, so let's harness our social power!"

It was that speaking opportunity that got me thinking about how to translate what I did at the White House into practical, everyday advice. Five women in the audience hired me to come speak at their organizations and offices over the next 10 months. At the end of that same year, my sister brought me as her guest to one of the city's most sought-after Christmas luncheon events. It's hosted annually by Sherren Leigh, one of Chicago's famous socialites and the founder of *Today's Chicago Woman* magazine. I was able to meet Sherren and so many other women that day over a selection of wines and delicious food at the famous Spiaggia restaurant, where President Obama and Michelle go for date night. I had a nice conversation with Sherren that day about the season, the current issue of her magazine and the fabulous women in attendance. I followed the event with a note of thanks and made sure to go out of my way each time I saw her at an event in the city.

Over the next four years, I got to know Sherren personally. My sister and I were profiled in *TCW's* sisters issue and we always supported Sherren's events for her foundation for women. In 2005, Sherren asked me to contribute to the magazine. So I did! I followed up with her editor the next day and started a column that ran for six months on "How to Eat, Drink and Get Mary A Job!" – a column that turned into the foundation for this very book! The exposure I received from *TCW* and Sherren led to more speaking opportunities, experience working with an editor and the groundwork for my future in writing.

By looking at the diagram of those closest to you, you can extend your reach double, triple and beyond. To help illustrate the power of social scenes, I turned to people in my own diagram to see how they built bridges that led to future success. In many cases, they found powerful opportunities where they least expected it. It was by being aware, being connected and punching in on that virtual clock that they were able to identify these chances and act on them.

Building the Inner Circle Bridge

IT WORKS! *Amy Van Ess, insurance agent in Plymouth, Wis., found a new career at a friend's funeral.*

"The father of one of my schoolmates passed away and, as a tradition goes, I went to pay respects at the visitation and deliver the traditional tuna casserole for the next week's lunch. After the church service, we all adjourned to the church basement for frosted Jell-Os and baked goods donated by friends and family. I was wandering from table to table catching up with people from my hometown when I ran into an old friend – and my future boss. At this stage in my life I had two small, school-aged children and was working nights managing a local restaurant and struggling to find time to help the kids with homework. My old friend and I chatted about how you always come back home to raise your family or just to be closer to parents. He explained that he was managing an insurance agency and thought I should send a resume and take the required testing to see if I would be a good match to become an insurance agent. My first thought was to be polite and play along. An insurance agent? Me? No way! But, I figured it couldn't hurt to take the test and was shocked when I got the highest score possible. I guess it was the career I am meant to have, or maybe it is the way I was raised. My father always said, if you get within three feet of someone, you should shake their hand, ask them their name and where they are from, figure out how you're related or who your mutual friends are, and how you can help!"

◆ CHILDREN ◆

Ah, children. I don't have any but many of my friends who are new parents often claim they have no life outside of the nursery. Some declare they lost their social scene once their first child was born, but they're discounting the powerful social scenes created *after* their child was born. Don't kid yourself; playgroups aren't just for the children. In fact, no matter what they say, a parent who spends $500 on their 3-year-old's birthday party for a clown, food and balloons to entertain other 3-year-olds is just as excited about having the parents of their child's friends visit, as they are about having given their kid a memorable birthday. Really, when you're a parent of a 3-year-old or 16-year-old, your social life revolves around that of your child – so take advantage of it. When you have children, there is always a social circle that goes with it, complete with new interests, friends and activities.

There are many bridges you can build through your child's events by simply sitting on a committee with fellow parents to plan the next school fundraiser or rooting your child on from the stands next to the other parents and the networks they represent! You can get as involved as you want for maximum return – both as a parent and master networker!

You will find many bridges to build within your Children social scene that will lead you to a parent who could be a potential client, partner or future employer. You spend hours with those parents, coaches and teachers at soccer practice every Saturday. Make the most of your time and get to know those around you!

Building the Children Bridge

IT WORKS! *Amy Carr, executive editor* **Time Out Chicago** *and Editor-in-chief* **Time Out Chicago Kids** *magazines found a business lead eating cupcakes with her kids.*

"As a magazine editor, I'm constantly on the lookout for good stories to tell our readers. Sometimes stories will come from a press release or an event, but the best stories usually come when you least expect it. That was certainly the case when I stumbled onto a great tip while attending a food allergy walk in Chicago with my family and friends. My 9-year-old son, Zach, suffers from a life-threatening peanut allergy. Dominic Guzzarde, the best friend of my oldest son, Carson, has the same condition. We've shared basketball games, Halloween parties, field trips and many, many allergy conversations with the Guzzarde family over the years. So it only made sense that we would also join them at the annual Food Allergy and Anaphylaxis Network walk in Lincoln Park. Though there's always a chance I might blog for timeoutchicago.com when I attend an event in the city, I wasn't wearing my editor's hat that day. I was a mom trying to learn more about an organization that could help my son, and hoping to increase awareness about a condition that affects 4 percent of all kids in the United States.

Many vendors had set up tables in the park to hand out allergen-free products, including Lisa Williams, who was handing out gluten-free cupcakes. Never one to turn down a cupcake, I began talking with Williams and learned she is a chef (and food allergy sufferer) who teaches classes on how to cook allergen-free. She also hosts Safe and Sound dinners where chefs at some of Chicago's top restaurants agree to cook allergen-free for a night. I took her business card, attended her next dinner at Boka and filed a lengthy blog post about it.

But we weren't finished there. Williams agreed to provide an in-home cooking class for the Guzzarde's and my kids. During the lesson, I learned Dominic nearly died after ingesting an egg roll fried in peanut oil years earlier, and that no one in the family had eaten Asian food since. Williams taught them how to make a safe, delicious Asian meal at home. I wrote about the experience and Williams for the Kids section of *Time Out Chicago*. I've since heard from many other parents who have similar stories and Mary Guzzarde has sent the article to nearly everyone she knows, many of whom could be potential new *TOC* readers. It's amazing how much can come from one little cupcake."

◆ NEIGHBORHOOD ◆

Whether you live in a high-rise or a quaint cul-de-sac like the Desperate Housewives, neighbors count! All you need is a front door to build a bridge to your neighbor's. My parents live on a cul-de-sac and they are always outside with the neighbors, helping each other out or having a beer in someone's garage. No matter where you take your daily walk in the neighborhood, there's a wealth of information to be learned and used that will benefit both your neighbor's lives and yours.

As for me, I live on the 12th floor of a condo building in Chicago. It may be 26 floors, but 12 is a neighborhood onto itself. There are seven units, seven individuals, seven different age groups, seven different jobs and seven different social diagrams. We have all become close; we've turned each other on to events and clubs; we have referred clients to each other; and we've expanded our businesses and lives by walking across each other's bridges. None of these bridges were found in a boardroom; they were discovered at our monthly round robins and birthday dinners. It all just happens naturally in our neighborhood setting. We aren't even close to our offices while we are at home doing great work!

Building the Neighborhood Bridge

IT WORKS! *Judith Schwartz, my mom and partner in my parent's photography studio, helped launch a new business at her annual garage sale.*

"Our neighborhood hosts a popular garage sale every summer to the point where we see repeat customers year after year! Julie, a petite woman who is just the right size for my daughter's suits, returns each year to build her wardrobe. The first year she stopped in, she didn't just buy the suits and leave. Instead she took the time to chat with me and through our conversation we talked about her being from China and my husband's and my photography studio. Julie said she was going back to China for a visit, and would stop in the studio when she got back to show us her photos from the trip. She came back with pictures, but also brought in some purses and jewelry she bought in China, and mentioned that she hoped to sell them here, but didn't know where to start. My husband and I gladly shared our contacts and ideas for certain consignment shops, gift stores and locations. Julie followed up on those ideas and started selling, ordered more merchandise and even began making her own. As demand for her merchandise grew she hired her daughter to help design and create the jewelry and even expanded into novelty shoes. She now has a 75-mile selling radius and has built a successful business, which started, you could say, out of our garage five years ago! Now I am the President of Plymouth Business Women and one of the first things I did was invite Julie to join and meet other business women who share ideas and bridges of their own."

◆ FAITH-BASED ORGANIZATIONS ◆

Faith-based organizations as a social scene? You bet. Everyone involved shares a common bond that can be the starting point for a relationship and a lifetime of bridge building.

Building the Faith-Based Bridge

IT WORKS! *Brenda Sexton, president and founder of chicagolink productions, found a powerful ally at church.*

"I had just moved back into Chicago from the suburbs after going through a divorce. My daughter was just 3 at the time and I wanted to find a church for the two of us to attend. I had been hearing great things about Old St. Pat's and its dynamic pastor Father Jack Wall. It is a Catholic church in the downtown area of Chicago that had been very close to closing up for good when the amazing and magnetic Jack Wall decided to invest his energy and determination into preserving it.

On my first visit, I went by myself, which felt a little uncomfortable, but I was courageous that day. After the service I introduced myself to Father Wall, and told him my young daughter and I had just moved back into the city. He was very cordial and welcoming.

The next Sunday I returned with my daughter in tow and after the service Father Wall came up to me and insisted that I meet Mayor Richard M. Daley and talk to him about my daughter attending the new school they were organizing at Old St. Pat's. So, how interesting was that? The mayor spent a good 20 minutes convincing me that I should enroll my daughter in this new school, which of course I did. I became friends with him and his wife, Maggie – in fact, she and I led the fundraising program at that school for years.

This connection led to my volunteering to work for Mayor Daley, who appointed me head of a committee to revitalize State Street, where I, of course, made further great connections in my field, which was commercial real estate at the time.

Sometimes, just showing up and taking the chance to expand your world brings great people and experiences into your life. Needless to say, this was a wonderful connection for me and got me further involved with my community and expanded my business."

◆ SERVICE ORGANIZATIONS ◆

Service organizations in every community offer an incredible opportunity to give back while gaining even more. Some groups require you to be sponsored by a current member; if you don't know a current member you can be paired up through a membership official. In most circumstances you don't need an invitation to join, just a commitment to attend meetings, volunteer at fundraisers and to spread the word about what the organization does and how it gives back.

Building the Service Bridge

IT WORKS! *Andréa Schwartz, my sister and regional vice president of media relations and cause marketing for Macy's, found a new career through her membership in the Junior league.*

"I had been teaching high school English for six years and spending the summers volunteering for presidential Press Advance through my sister at the White House when I realized that I wanted to change careers from teaching to public relations and the media. Though I taught at a high school out in the suburbs, I lived in Chicago and it was important to me to build a group of friends in my neighborhood. I joined the Junior League of Chicago to expand my circle of friends and to volunteer in their various service projects with the youth and women of the city. Outside of service projects we had a lot of fun events, galas, parties and cocktail receptions, which gave us a wonderful opportunity to meet each other. When I decided to make the move from teaching, I announced it at a cocktail reception to let everyone know that I was looking for a position in communications. One of my fellow members, to my surprise, was the shoe buyer at one of America's first department stores and icon of Chicago, Marshall Field's. She found me during the reception to tell me that she thought there was a position open in their public relations department. The next day she called me to say that there was indeed an opening for a public relations specialist and got me in contact with the head of the department. I was hired for that position 13 years ago and today am proud to be the vice president of media relations and cause marketing for Macy's North and Midwest Regions. It was through the bridge that the Junior League of Chicago provided for me as I took an active role in the organization and built friendships with the members that led to where I am professionally today!"

♦ CHARITY AND NONPROFIT ♦ ORGANIZATIONS

Sweet charity! My favorite. Much like the events you attend and participate in with a service organization, you have those fabulous galas, carnivals and 5Ks for charity. This scene includes many incredible people from different backgrounds representing many things – all coming together for a cause. Which makes for a strong foundation to build a relationship into a partnership. Over a four-course dinner you can get to know a lot about those seated around you, what you can do for them where they can be of help for you. It's always nice to have something in common, and an excuse to go meet someone who normally won't return your phone calls. This can be a wonderful opportunity to "bump" into someone who you have wanted to meet so long, as long as you proceed with tact (more on that later). Rest assured, this scene is a win-win situation, for yourself and your charity.

Building my Charity Bridge

I got involved with the American Heart Association in 2006 when I attended the Go Red for Women Luncheon at Navy Pier in Chicago. Having lost three grandparents to heart disease and well aware that heart disease is the No. 1 killer of women, I was motivated to get involved. I gathered all the information I could and have increased my involvement since with their Heart Balls and luncheons. Over the last three years, I have donated silent auction items, shown up at every event and was asked to serve on the AHA Advocacy Committee working with local, state and national legislatures to improve heart disease and stroke survival rates and resources. When asked, I didn't look at the committee as optional; I looked at it as an opportunity to get further involved, meet more advocates, build bridges for fellow members of the AHA and work on behalf of the victims and survivors of heart disease.

After my second committee meeting, Jeanette Flom, the

vice president of corporate development, asked me to come speak to her. She had seen me in action at the meeting and wanted me to emcee the AHA Heart Walks, which are among their biggest community events of the year! I was honored to be asked and had a ball! Over two weekends and four walks, I was in front of more than 25,000 people and met wonderful families walking in memory and honor of their loved ones. I was able to talk with them not just from the stage but one on one at the finish line about the incredible programs and resources of the AHA. The organization changes lives and it has changed my life for the better. I even got a call from a walker who wants me to come speak to her company – not to mention a nice guy who wants a date! It's amazing how helping someone or being involved in an organization ends up changing your life as well – professionally and personally!

◆   CLUBS AND LEAGUES   ◆

Whether it's the gym, a wine club or the golf course, clubs are about more than just getting in shape, finding a fabulous pinot noir or making par. These are clubs that revolve around a social atmosphere, but it's up to you to turn that social talk into something productive! I'm all for keeping things light and fun (you don't want to bring people down on craft night talking about your problems; you want to find out what is happening in their lives!). You want to find bridges in your own social scenes that can help them get to where they're going. After all, isn't that what the 19th hole is all about?

Building the Club and League Bridge

IT WORKS! *Hedy Ratner, co-president and founder of the Women's Business Development Center in Chicago built her bridge to Oprah at the gym.*

"For the organization's 20th anniversary I was determined to have the inspirational Oprah Winfrey address the 2,000 women at our annual conference. But no matter how many letters I sent and phone calls I made to Oprah's office, I received only a polite rejection or no response. Unwilling to accept defeat, I looked for other ways to get to Oprah, namely at the East Bank Club, which was where Oprah often worked out and where I also worked out! Oprah hadn't spoken to a large group in Chicago for well over a decade and at best, she was a long shot. In one desperate gesture, several months before our 20th anniversary conference, I saw Oprah working out on a treadmill and carefully positioned myself nearby. I blurted out something like, 'I run the Women's Business Development Center. It's the oldest and largest women's business assistance center in the U.S. We are celebrating our 20th anniversary at our conference in September and I have been trying for 20 years to bring you in as keynote speaker. It's your 20th anniversary as well and I will have 2,000 women business owners attending and I want you to be our speaker.' And lo and behold she responded that she would be willing if she is available on that date and told me to call such and such a person to make arrangements. Though Oprah couldn't commit, with a name in hand,

I was able to call Oprah's office one more time to say, 'Oprah wanted me to call you,' and, ultimately, I landed the world's most powerful TV talk show host as the keynote speaker for our conference. And she rocked!"

◆ COLLEGE ◆

You're not just going to college for an academic foundation; this is a perfect opportunity for you to build a "social foundation," as well. College is based on one social event after another. Study groups and the cafeteria are where everyone goes to find out which professors are good, easy or bad, who's hooking up with whom and where the best party that night will be. You may not realize it but as a student you are already using "social" functions" to find out valuable information. In the workplace and life after college you will still be using similar social events for information, only then you'll be focusing on who's getting promoted and who's getting fired more than who is hosting the Saturday night kegger. It's all social – just different goals. There are endless opportunities to hone your networking skills in college!

Building my College Bridge

Though I never finished college, it is still how I got my start at the White House. While I was a freshman and first semester sophomore at St. Norbert College in DePere, Wis., I was involved in everything social, as well as academic. Sure, I had good grades but most importantly I built strong relationships with the professors who, in turn, became my mentors. Socially,

I was everywhere, from being on the College Activities Board and involved in the Residence Social Association and the C.C. Hams independent sorority, and of course I spent my share of time at the Abby Bar. Through my social events, along with the relationships I built with the faculty, I learned about the Washington Semester Program at the American University. It wasn't posted anywhere, so I never would have heard about it if not for my close ties with my communications professor, who advised me to pursue it. That opportunity was what first brought me to the door of the White House and forever changed my life!

◆ OFFICE ◆

The office may seem like the opposite of a social scene, but what about around that water cooler? What about those birthday parties in the afternoon, office-sponsored happy hours, conventions, sales meetings, client dinners, seminars and breakfasts. What about your coffee buddy who walks with you to the Starbucks every afternoon for that caffeine pick me up. All of these office-created functions are places to find out where bridges may exist for you or someone you work with. You're not just grabbing coffee with a colleague before a meeting – you're finding opportunities to learn their social diagram and discover where yours can fit together.

Building the Office Bridge

IT WORKS! *Jennifer King, a consumer product tester from Neenah, found a job at her husband's company picnic.*

"My husband Jason works for a printing company and every year they host a summer picnic for the employees and their families. We had just moved to a new city and I had given birth to my second child. While at the picnic I spoke with lots of my husband's co-workers and spouses. One of the women I spoke with had mentioned to me a company nearby specializes in consumer trials and suggested I contact them about participating with my son in a diaper trial. Yes, diapers. They paid me to evaluate the diapers on a daily basis in my home – which meant I never had to pay for my son's diapers! After that trial, it lead to another and another. When my son started going to school I became a full-time consumer product tester. It's terrific to have the second income and it all started at an office picnic!"

◆ PROFESSIONAL ORGANIZATIONS ◆

Professional organizations and industry associations are often designed to be networked in the sense of "what can you do for me/my business." But you can go beyond building bridges just for yourself and your company; this is a great opportunity to be the "B," aka, the connector. Be known as the person who can get people to anyone or anything. These situations are natural for networking, as everyone expects to talk about what they do for a living and what they can do to help others. However, you can go a step beyond. When you're attending a dinner at an annual conference or a "networking" happy hour, get to know these folks for more than who they represent; get to know them for who they are and what they "like" to do and where they do it. You will find that they have bridges to where someone you know needs to go or where you want to go yourself!

Building the Professional Organization Bridge

IT WORKS! *Olivia Luk, an attorney at Jenner and Block LLC, created contacts in a new city using professional organization ties from her past.*

"In 2006, I moved from Washington, D.C., to Chicago to marry my law school sweetheart. Since I had established six years worth of professional relations in D.C., I worried about starting over and losing my connections.

In D.C., I was actively involved in a professional association called the "Giles S. Rich American Inn of Court." Members included judges, professors, attorneys and law students interested in intellectual property law who gather monthly to promote civility, ethics and professionalism. Most meetings consist of a program followed by a dinner or reception where members "break bread" while networking. I was lucky to have Circuit Judge Richard Linn of the U.S. Court of Appeals for the Federal Circuit as a mentor, as my "B," my connector.

The day I moved to Chicago to join a global law firm in the patent litigation group, I put a plan into action to start a new "Inn of Court" in Chicago specializing in intellectual property law. I was lucky to have Judge Linn's support. He connected me with the most influential and active members of the intellectual property bar. Within three short years, what I created as "The Richard Linn American Inn of Court" has more than 150 members and received the Circle of Excellence distinction from the National Inns of Court. I also founded the Linn Inn Alliance with Judge Linn to assist with starting new intellectual property Inns across the nation.

The power of professional networking over wine and hors d'oeuvres should not be discounted. I would never have met most of the intellectual property bar in Chicago – from students to judges to young attorneys to the most established partners – had I not sacrificed non-billable hours to meet, have drinks with, have dinner with and work with Inn members on programs. Now I have an incredible professional social network, many of whom I count as my closest friends."

◆ CITY AND COMMUNITY ◆

One thing we all have in common is a place where we live and pay taxes...so why not get involved in your city? Take advantage of the concerts in the park, movie night and sidewalk sales, not just to support the event but to meet those who attend. These are residents who work and live in your city. Get to know those that are sitting around you; you never know who you'll meet. You may find bridges you can build for them, or they may build a bridge for you to walk across someday.

Building the City and Community Bridge

IT WORKS! *Julienne Gohde, a team manager for Tastefully Simple, found friends and a side job by joining a group.*

"My husband Steve and I moved to Oshkosh, Wis., four years ago. Steve works for the city and I'm a Tastefully Simple Team Manager and stay-at-home mom with our two children. When I moved here I didn't know a single soul, so I joined the Oshkosh Newcomers Group as a way to meet people and learn about opportunities in the city. Not only did I make great new friends and find play dates for my children, I started hosting Tastefully Simple taste testing parties in some of their homes! It was a wonderful way for me to develop my business in a new city. One of the newcomers even signed up with me as a Tastefully Simple consultant! Choosing to get involved in the city was a profitable decision!"

◆ POLITICAL AND CIVIC ACTION ◆ ORGANIZATIONS

Nothing brings out a common passion like politics and civic action groups! This is another social scene that establishes a common bond between you and others who show up for a meeting, rally or fundraiser. It's a great way to gain access to the political decision-makers of your city, state and federal government, and meet those who have their ear. In fact, here is another example of an event where you don't need an invitation to attend. Do your due diligence as a guest, which we will learn later in the Dress Rehearsal chapter, and find out who will be there, especially if you are looking for someone in particular.

Building the Political and Civic Action Organizations Bridge

IT WORKS! *Letty Hudson, CEO of Chicago Mini Bus Travel Inc., made a powerful political contact in an elevator.*

"Recently I was in Washington, D.C., for the Women In Public Policy annual legislative meeting. As I was listening to the different speakers, one in particular caught my attention. She worked in health-care reform and spoke about her weekly meetings with President Obama and specifically what they were trying to achieve to make an impact on how American's health recovery is being treated. I right away knew she would be a great contact for Neli Vazquez-Rowland, co-founder of A Safe Haven. I am such a fan of A Safe Haven that I carry Neli's DVDs and brochures on their recovery centers to pass out to assist her in getting their message to key people in the D.C. area. As the speaker was leaving, I followed behind and rode with her on the elevator. During the ride, I introduced myself to her, thanked her for taking the time to speak with the organization, and spoke to her about A Safe Haven. I left her with some literature and a DVD. Though she couldn't make a commitment to get involved on the spot, I could take her card back to Neli, for her to follow up. I was able to build a bridge for Neli and A Safe Haven by taking an active role in a civic action committee. "

◆ SOCIAL NETWORKING SITES ◆
AND BLOGS

For obvious reasons, the Internet is a "virtual" social scene. Facebook not only reconnects you with old friends, it can connect you with new ones and start a conversation. Although at some point you'll want to move that conversation from e-mails to instant messaging to an actual face-to-face meeting, Facebook is a great place to start. I also like Facebook and other social networking sites for research. If I have a nice conversation with someone new and want to help them professionally or personally, I can check out their Facebook page, look at their information, their friends or, in the case of LinkedIn, their connections, and find where I overlap or have the bridge for them to get to where they want to go. Social networking sites are also a great tool when becoming a powerful guest (See the next section!).

Blogs are another community of not just information but people. Perhaps you share a common bond over subject matter that you both are blogging about? Maybe you comment on the same blog posts. Through this virtual connection, you can build bridges that could be mutually beneficial.

No matter what social networking tool you prefer, it's a good idea to decide if your profile will be business, personal or business with a little background information about your hobbies. Think about creating two accounts so that your status at the dance club doesn't show up on the wall of a potential client. Invite friends to certain accounts and potential clients and business associates to another. When you use and post on multiple networks, maximize your time and virtually connect as many as possible so you have crossover status updates and address books across each platform. Lastly, when listing your profile information make it as complete and professional as possible. It's still a resume; it's just on a "social" networking site instead of stationery! Don't let it fool you into thinking otherwise!

Building the Social Networking Bridge

IT WORKS! *Christine Childers, a bankruptcy lawyer in Chicago, found a new client through her Facebook profile.*

"During law school, I was a member of the Christian Legal Society and even served as vice president of Valparaiso Law School's law student chapter. After law school, I continued my membership in CLS virtually through their social networking site and website. I hadn't had much opportunity to get involved on a local level, but by listing my CLS membership on my biography and Facebook page, a client found me. This particular client needed bankruptcy counsel in Chicago and told his counsel in another state that he wanted a Christian bankruptcy lawyer. With a simple search on the Internet, my firm biography was located and I was hired by the client – simply as a result of my continued involvement with CLS and listing that involvement on my social networking pages and company website."

THE BOTTOM LINE

Your social scenes are as powerful as you want to make them! It is up to you to look into and diagram each of your scenes to find places for you to build bridges, and, where they already exist, find opportunities for you to cross. You will find some of your bridges are in your existing scenes and other bridges will be built in scenes you need to develop and add to your diagram. Once you do that, it's off to becoming the most powerful guest you can be. The extent to which you productively use your social scenes to network will depend on your actions as a "guest." And who doesn't love being on the "A" list!

THE POWER
OF THE GUEST

WE HAVE LEARNED social scenes can be found in both our professional and personal communities. When they overlap, their power can double, even quadruple. But we can't take advantage of the scene unless we know and understand the power we as guests bring to it. Because as social as any event may appear, it is business, but whether it is powerful is in the hands of you, the guest.

These powers will mean the difference between being noticed or blending in, obtaining a promotion vs. being passed over, climbing the ladder of success vs. standing at the bottom waiting for someone to wave you up. I'm going to lay out everything for you. Once you've learned to find the right event, get invited and prepare for that day, you'll be ready to unleash your power at any so-called "social" event.

◆ WORK THE ROOM ◆

At one time or another we have all noticed someone at an event who seems to have total control of the room. They are the ones who exude a certain confidence, but not superiority. They move smoothly among the guests and each conversation, put everyone at ease and appear effortless as they work the room. They do all of this while staking their place in the company, positioning themselves for a promotion, acquiring a new client, achieving a place in the community, raising money for charity, or securing a place for their children in the school they want them to attend. No goal is out of reach at the right social event once you realize and exercise the power you possess as a guest.

Although it may look "effortless," what you don't see is the preparation that takes place before the guest even walks through the door. A powerful guest knows who they will be surrounded by, how they can influence other guests and what they want to accomplish before they even check their coat. Their power stems from how they appear physically and mentally, who they appear with (if anyone at all), how they are introduced, how they converse, and ultimately how they follow up. These powerful guests have control over each one of these variables. Soon, you will, too.

◆ WHO CAN BECOME ◆ A POWERFUL GUEST?

These powers can be applied to anyone — the lives of the powerful executive, established entrepreneur, young associate, aspiring politician, struggling actor, soccer mom, Junior Leaguer or college student and beyond. You do not have to have a type "A" personality to use these powers. You only need to be ready to become a guest who can turn a social situation into a ticket to meeting someone who otherwise wouldn't return your call. This is what the power of the guest is all about – using what you might think is an "ordinary social event" to attain something much more beneficial than just free food and drink.

◆ THE PREP ◆

What we experience over two hours of an award-winning film is the result of years of preparation! Those hours are a mere fraction of the hard work, time and effort put in by the producers, writers, director, actors, location scouts, stunt coordinators and even wardrobe! All of the decisions and preparations for a film are finished before the camera is loaded and the director shouts…"Action!" Just as a movie comes together, your networking power builds as you prepare for any event!

The ideal location is vital to any film scene. Similarly, you need to find events in your social scenes that provide the ideal setting to build bridges for yourself and others. "Casting Calls" are open auditions that can list where, when and what kind of actors or other guests will be present!

Once you get the role or "invitation," it's time to go into Dress Rehearsals. This is your time to get familiar with your role and those of the other actors. Time in rehearsal determines how well received your performance will be and how effectively you will be able to relay your message to your audience…your fellow guests.

◆ THE PAYOFF ◆

Then it's on to "Showtime" where all your preparation comes together and allows you to shine! You'll be able to hit your marks, meet those you want to speak with, start building bridges, relationships and partnerships. All because of your preparation before you even walk through the door!

Of course, after a show when audience members are brought to their feet, you want to keep them there shouting "Encore! Encore!" You need to focus on the follow up and follow through with your new and continuing relationships. And just like a film or live performance is reviewed, this is the time for you to critique your own performance and evaluate what worked and what should be changed for the next event. Continue to improve your performance every time.

Of course, there are major differences between preparing for the stage or screen vs. real life. You are not playing a character; however, you can build on your character and career. You can work at networking and learn to become a more powerful guest!

The culmination of your efforts will allow you to **Eat, Drink and Succeed!**

THE
CASTING CALL

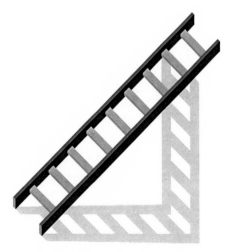

IN THIS AGE OF REALITY TV, an open casting call for *American Idol* is considered the ultimate job fair. You can do better. There are plenty of events that will put you center stage and give you a chance to step into the spotlight. You don't need TV cameras to make the most of your own reality – just a wide net and a fresh outlook to help you find the part that's right for you.

In this chapter, you're the one holding the audition. The goal is to cast yourself at an event filled with people and opportunities that will help you Eat, Drink and Succeed. Once you find the right event, your critical eye will help you identify the perfect cast members for the reality show of your dreams. These casting calls will help prepare you for when the tables turn and you find yourself auditioning for a promotion or a new client. You're ready to be a star, but first you need the proper stage.

♦ THE POWER OF THE EVENT ♦

If you look for it, you can find power in any event. Anytime people are gathered together in any atmosphere, there's powerful potential to build a bridge, find a deal, make a deal or even make amends in a forgiving atmosphere.

Any atmosphere? Yes! It's as simple as choosing to sit next to someone new on a shuttle during an annual conference where you have the potential to change a life – and that might be yours! Looking at your social diagram and your life's activities, you can see that events come in all shapes and sizes with all kinds of guest lists. It can be a gala, football game, business luncheon, conference keynote, cocktail party, 5K charity run, gallery show or neighborhood barbecue. The list of potentially powerful events is endless. There are no parameters to set because when more than one are gathered together – whether there is wine on the table at a dinner or water in your bottles at the gym – these are all exceptional social events that can be powerful if you choose to take advantage!

♦ THE POWER OF THE INVITATION ♦

Whether it's an engraved classic, a handwritten note or an evite, each invitation is powerful. Sure, we respond faster to the invite that is hand-delivered attached to a bottle of champagne, but the spur-of-the-moment get-together shouldn't dissuade us from finding the power. The invitation is your ticket. Think *Willy Wonka and the Chocolate Factory* and the Golden Ticket! This is your passport to get into the event and it holds all the information you need to find its power.

Many events have potential to be powerful and some hosts are great at designing them with this in mind. Your challenge is to find a way to make it powerful for *you*. The invitation gives you all the clues you need to investigate whether the event will be a good combination of people and place. Perhaps the event is at a location you have just always wanted an excuse to visit, or a way into an exclusive venue. The key to how powerful you make the event will be in your research. Just as an actor must rehearse for opening night in the role that could make him a star, you need to do your homework in advance. The invitation is the foundation for you to build your game plan. So put that invitation in a safe place, you're going to need it ahead!

◆ NO CRASHING! ◆

You want to work your way up the ladder – not fall off! No couple has fallen off harder and faster than Tareq and Michaele Salahi, the White House party crashers who in late 2009 managed to get into the Indian State Dinner. The stars aligned for the Salahis that night when the usually flawless Secret Service did not properly compare their names to those on the approved list *and* the White House Social Office wasn't at the point of entry to check their names off its list! All of the players in that scenario lost credibility. Keep your credibility in tact *with* tact! If you're not invited, get an invitation, and if you can't, choose another event!

◆ GET INVITED! ◆

We all have "automatic" events in our professional and personal lives. Office parties, happy hours, annual conferences, client dinners, birthday parties, school functions, etc. But it's time to think out of the box, or in some cases, the cubicle. There are hundreds of events out there every day in small and large communities alike, just waiting to be tapped into. Now's your chance to start auditioning social events that could change your life, professionally and personally.

◆ FREE CITY MAGAZINES, NEWSPAPERS, ONLINE RESOURCES CONFERENCE PROGRAMS ◆

I live in Chicago and on every corner of the city you see free newspapers and magazines. On the average street corner you will find everything from apartment guides, quick weight loss programs, how to make money at home and my favorite magazines *Chicago Social, Today's Chicago Woman, Michigan Avenue* and *Chicago Magazine,* as well as my local neighborhood newspapers. You've got these resources in your neighborhoods, too, both literally and virtually. So often we walk past these "advertisements" and don't even give them a second look unless we have a long bus ride and nothing else to do. But once you realize the powerful opportunities lurking inside, you'll make it a habit to start looking at these potential gold mines regularly.

Let's start with *CS* magazine. *CS* stands for Chicago Social and it contains about 100 pages of everything from fashion trends, advertisements, local commerce profiles, special interest articles, society party photographs and a priceless calendar filled with every social event that is happening in the next month. It publishes five-to-10 pages a month listing upcoming events in the city. Next to each date in bold is the name, organization, sponsor, co-chairs, sometimes the name of an honoree and price of the event. In fact, each year they publish a *CS* Charity Datebook with a listing of all the events for the year ahead! And remember, when it comes to the price of the event, especially the gala fundraisers, it typically includes, at the very least, cocktails if not a full dinner and dance. As an added bonus, a portion is usually tax deductible! Most of the events are held to benefit the organization or person being honored with proceeds going to charity. Talk to your accountant for details, but remember charity for others can also be a benefit for yourself.

Another secret tool found in publications like CS magazine and SPLASH, a society-focused section of the Chicago Sun-Times, are the photos of last month's events. Even if you didn't make it to all, or any, of them, you are able to see the pictures highlighting the people (names in caption) who were together for a good cause or person in the community. Just as I used the White House staff directory to familiarize myself with key players in D.C., you can take a photo tip sheet like this one and familiarize yourself with the social scene in your own town. *Today's Chicago Woman* has these sections, as well, and even the small community newspapers have a page for benefit listings and events. In Chicago, some of these newspapers are the *Downtown Loop* for the Michigan Avenue area, *The Windy City Times* for the gay and lesbian communities and the *Chicago Defender* for the African-American community. These types of publications, which target a niche audience, are a powerful place to look for events that fit your specific goals.

By far my favorite Internet resource for events in any city is arts and entertainment magazine *Time Out* (timeout.com) and for me that means *Time Out Chicago*. The *Time Out* brand has extended its reach to 33 cities in 25 countries worldwide and now even publishes *Time Out Kids* in some cities. So, for those parents who build their social life around their children, this is a great resource for you! Remember, their scene is also your scene.

Time Out is tailor-made to fit any social life – or lack thereof. Log on to timeoutchicago.com and the first thing you'll see is an area to click for "What's Going On,""Five Things To Do Today" and a section for free events. There is no excuse not to find an event that could be powerful!

You expect to find valuable opportunities at business conferences, but many people overlook an incredibly powerful tool: the conference program. How many times have you scanned the schedule to learn what time the general sessions start and which evening activities you can skip to meet up with your friends in the area? Next time you attend a meeting, make the most of the conference program by using it to make connections during scheduled free time. Make a commitment to get to the continental breakfast early and to leave your phone in your pocket, leaving one hand for your coffee and the other free to shake a hand. Sessions, luncheons, dinners and shuttles rides to off-site activities all present chances to sit with and meet someone new or to continue a conversation from earlier in the day. These are all easily overlooked opportunities, but they are just as important as the general sessions and expo itself!

◆ GET INVOLVED! ◆

For a great automatic in, join an organization or industry association that sponsors a lot of the activities and events you want to attend. Maybe it's the people they attract or their commitment to a specific cause that you are interested in. Either reason is a good one because you will find more event opportunities, meet different people (and their friends) and have access to their social diagrams, which will expand your personal and professional circles.

Getting involved in an organization is not only a great way to get invited to various events, but a way to get a head start and save some money. Let's say that you volunteer to work the seating arrangements. This is no small task, especially when seating a 600-person dinner, but it is all worth it in the end when you sit yourself at a table for several hours next to someone from whom you could benefit! Or volunteer to work at the check-in table. You get to greet each guest as they arrive. If their name is one you want to get to know, make a note of what they are wearing and look like so you can find them later. And take note, if you volunteer on an event committee, you and a guest usually get to attend for free!

For example, when I lived in Washington, D.C., I was asked to serve on the Larry King Cardiac Foundation Gala Committee. When I met with the director of the foundation to get involved, he mentioned that not only would I have the opportunity to serve with prominent people from various professional communities, but as a thank you, my guest and I would receive complimentary tickets worth $350 a piece to enjoy the gala. In the end, I was able to meet some great people, some of whom I am still friends with today. I also made some very productive relationships with guests I met at the gala and, better yet, had the opportunity to work for a cause in which I believe.

What are the local groups or industry associations you would be interested in joining? There are many possibilities including professional organizations for every profession like the Global Business Travel Association, National Association of Women Business Owners, American Hotel and Lodging Association, the National Association of Home Builders, International Special Events Society, Meeting Planners International and their local chapters for day to day involvement and interaction. There are young professional groups like The Young Presidents' Organization; service organizations like the Lion's, Rotary or Kiwanis clubs; political organizations such as the city or county chapters of the Democratic and Republican parties; religious organizations such as your church's board of trustees and your local chapter of the Jewish Federation of America; and private clubs such as the New York Athletic Club, the University Club or the Metropolitan Club of Chicago with shared memberships between clubs worldwide.

The list of groups in every professional and personal community around the country is endless. When you look around at your own community calendar you will see what is out there! Don't forget, a lot of the dues for various organizations are tax deductible and membership in an organization gives you the opportunity to attend an event you may not otherwise be able to afford.

I encourage you to diversify your involvement in these organizations. Professional organizations are great for your career, but community organizations can be just as powerful because their events are popular with people from all different social scenes. They give us a chance to create a common denominator with a sea of guests who could be our ticket into a new job or career opportunity.

Once you have found the right event in your Casting Call it's time to build your character. It's time for Dress Rehearsal.

DRESS REHEARSAL

ON THE STAGE, rehearsal is necessary to guarantee success. Actors study the screenplay or script and develop their characters. For you, dress rehearsal is where you build on your character and move yourself into position to get the most out of any event you attend! This is where you do all of your preparation so when you walk onto the set – a happy hour, black tie, office party, annual conference or the first hole on the golf course – you already know what scenes will take place and you're ready to hit your mark.

When you hear "Showtime," you'll be ready because of your "Dress Rehearsal." In this chapter, you'll learn the techniques and tools needed to earn rave reviews, and maybe that well-deserved promotion or new job. It's important to prepare for your role as a smart networker, because you are not the only performer going on stage. Also remember, there is always an understudy waiting to take your part! You want a flawless performance, and it all starts in rehearsal.

◆ THE POWER OF RESEARCH ◆

Researching an event can guarantee your success and level of credibility before you even set foot inside the venue. Remember, the unrehearsed actor gets booed off the stage and is rarely heard from again, but a talented and hard-working star earns legions of fans.

We have all watched James Bond use his investigative tools to save the world from evil villains. Now, it is *your* time to investigate because, while evil may not be lurking around the corner, your professional life still hangs in the balance. You've already done some research on the event when you decided to attend. But before you set foot inside the door, it pays to undertake a much more in-depth study.

President Bill Clinton never went into an event un-prepared. He expected a briefing memo for every event by 7:30 p.m. the night before, whether it was a small dinner, State Dinner, bill signing or White House Carnival.

Sometimes that meant two, three or even four memos a night just from me. Each brief would contain information on the event, its purpose, background on the policy or announcements being made or discussed, detailed information on each program participant, and a description of the audience and folks expected to be in attendance. That was in addition to the basics of location, time and attire – all incredibly important. So why not prepare yourself like the most powerful person in the world?

Just like the President's three-ring, leather-bound Briefing Book with its presidential seal, you should have a notebook that includes your research. Let's walk through it step by step.

Who?

Who is the host, host company or organization?
Who are your fellow guests and honorees?

Next time you have a break in your day, instead of looking up viral videos, go online and look up information on the host(s) of your next event, fellow guests and the companies and organizations they represent. Get his or her bio, look at the corporation or business he or she works for, scour the business section of newspaper websites and pay particular attention to headlines that may be of interest, including the company's daily performance on the New York Stock Exchange. The Internet is a huge resource, and when in doubt, just go to Google. If you can't find anything on the Internet, go ahead and call the person's office and ask for a bio or, better yet, create your own version of "Six Degrees of Kevin Bacon" by playing "Six Degrees of 'X' CEO." You can find out the kind of person this is through people who have had a personal connection to him or his company.

If the event is a charity benefit for a specific cause, go to the event or charity website before the function to find out the mission statement and background of the organization, its funding and the list of directors or members of the governing body. This allows you to identify a connection you can make or discover one you already have within the organization. If you found out one of the honorees is being honored because of his work with the organization "Operation Smile," make sure you look at the website so you can not only congratulate that honoree, but ask some questions or start a dialogue on the organization/reason he is being honored. This will show that person that you're not simply saying congratulations, you're telling them you know why they deserved to be congratulated. It will open up your conversation to discuss their life, work and how there may be bridges you can provide, or that they have for you to cross.

What else can you find out about the "who," whether it's the host or guest? You can research with whom they have been involved, such as a business merger or industry association. Find out where your fellow guests have worked. Where did they go to school? What did they study? What was/is their career path and what former positions have they held? On the personal side, you should find out if these guests are single, married with or without children. And never forget to find out what their spouses do. Sometimes it's not the primary guest that may be of interest to you, but perhaps their spouse can lend a hand in a professional or personal aspiration.

Answering these questions on the "Who" before you get to the event will give you conversation topics, alert you to danger zones and allow you to more effectively prepare for meeting someone with whom you would like to do business, or whose friendship you are interested in. Take the time to gather your information; it will be the difference between getting to meet someone and getting to *know* someone at an event. If you can get to know the host or guests' interests and pastimes before you leave for the event, you will have another tool in your toolbox of conversation topics.

So ask yourself these questions: Are any of the people invited, people you would like to do business with or meet? Is there a bridge you can build for someone attending? Would your presence at the event and meeting any of these people possibly enhance your professional/personal status in your community? Are any of the companies interesting to you professionally? Is there someone attending the event you could mingle with who can introduce you to another person you normally wouldn't be able to meet. Could this event be the key to unlocking that elusive office door?

What?
What is the event?

Is it a fundraiser, anniversary celebration, movie premiere, merger announcement, annual conference, political endorsement, a children's sports banquet or church picnic? What is the common bond that ties the event to the guests? Is it a common belief in a charitable cause or political candidate, a hand in the longevity of a corporation or couple, a love of movies, association with their church or school? And how does the involvement of fellow guests compare with your own personal or professional involvement?

By asking yourself these questions, you can establish a commonality or rapport with your fellow guests before you arrive. Use it as an opening into a conversation that could lead to a professional partnership or other beneficial relationship.

When?
When is the event?

Is the event day or night? A weekday or weekend? What time of day is the event taking place – is it a breakfast, lunch, tea, cocktails, dinner, gala or dessert reception? The day of the week and time of day can indicate the formality or opportunity this event holds as you prepare to "work" the room. You can assume that a seated dinner will be preceded by a cocktail hour, which allows you an opportunity to mingle. Even after dinner you may be able to catch up with guests you were not seated near. A luncheon on a weekday, however, may be more structured, leaving less time for small-talk and the need for more creativity.

Investigating the "when" will help you create your game plan and, as you'll see later, prepare you for your Power of Appearance, as well.

Where?
Where is the event?

Can you get to it? Do other arrangements have to be made? Do you have to weigh its potential power against the cost of a plane ticket or an evening or day away from your home or office? What relevance does the site hold for the event's purpose?

Sometimes events are held at interesting locations of historical or cultural importance. Call the event location ahead of time and see if they have a website or any printed information on the history of the venue. Instead of relying on the latest weather prediction, this information can serve as an easy conversation opener while impressing others and giving you credibility at the same time.

A potential client of mine recently called me up and invited me to a beautiful restaurant in Chicago. Having heard of the restaurant but never having been there, I took the time to Google it and checked out its website. I not only was able to look at and choose what I would order off the menu, but I also checked around the site for background on the location and restaurant itself. I found an interesting story about the art that hangs in the dining room and the artist. Wow, did I impress my table when I was able to point out the paintings and talk about their relevance to the restaurant. The five minutes of research on the location and restaurant was priceless and I locked in the client. I have seen those clients since and they always tell me they love to repeat the stories of the artwork whenever they dine there. Which means they always think of me when they eat there. I'd say that's a pretty good way to positively get into someone's head – even when you're not with them!

Why?
Why should you attend the event?

Would this event offer a chance for you to meet someone at the bar or buffet who you would not ordinarily be able to meet at his or her workplace? Remember, at a charity event there are no personal assistants telling you that the boss is on the other line or "out of the office." Look to your social diagram and find places where this event could build bridges for you and for others through you.

This is where your investigation on the "who" will pay off. You can effectively weigh the "why" because you have already investigated the who, what, when and where, and are able to assess the opportunity you have to increase your professional or personal value.

How?

How can you use this event for more than
just the free food and drink?

How can you turn this ordinary party into a powerful opportunity to impress a boss, colleague or friend? How can you use this event to meet someone you can't manage to meet any other way?

Remember, if you can get your foot in the door with a company executive by taking a seat next to her at the bar or conveniently ending up next to her at the buffet, you now have an opportunity to converse. Make your move to conversation an educated one. Your conversation, backed by proper investigation, will not only get you noticed, but can lead you into his or her corner office, as well.

Putting It All to Work

Through the Power of Research, you slowly unravel the mystery of the event and it suddenly becomes much larger and more promising than it first appeared. When you have completed your research and compiled your briefing book, you can make an informed decision on whether this function could be a powerful one. Then make your list of people you want to meet and be ready to initiate interesting conversation and meet your goals.

THE BOTTOM LINE

We research our choices when selecting professions, schools, a child's day care, romantic partners and job prospects. Why not research social opportunities, as well? Take the invitation or article about the event and break it down using the charity/organization's name; sponsor, if one is listed; the names of the co-chairs; honoree; and price of the event. Then get to a computer and get started.

◆ THE POWER OF KNOWLEDGE ◆

Knowledge *is* power. Your research will have educated you on the Who, What, When, Where, Why and How of the event, but it must be supplemented with everyday information and current events to make you *knowledgeable*. For a clear advantage at any event, you should constantly keep current on a wide range of topics – an easy task in the Internet age. Through your Power of Knowledge, you can walk into and "work" any room because you are prepared for conversation on anything. By being well-versed in a variety of subjects, you will appear both credible and impressive because of your ability to interact as an active participant on many topics, not just a few.

There are some easy ways to make a credible impression! And it all starts with the basics. For example, during my seminars

I ask for a show of hands on how many people have read any newspaper online or in print on that given day. Usually, about 50 percent of hands are raised. Then I proceed to ask questions on the specific sections of the paper. Who read the front page and first section, which is usually dedicated to local news and national topics of importance?; about 70 percent of the 50 percent. Who read the business section?; about 50 percent. Who read sports?; about 40 percent, and of that 90 percent are male. Who read the arts and entertainment section?; about 30 percent and of that 95 percent female. We really don't think about it when we are reading the paper, in terms of gathering news in specific areas of interest; that if we read a little of each story we are learning things that may be interesting to a variety of people. Contrary to popular belief, events and conversation are not just about us. By reading even the front page of each section, including business, sports, entertainment/style and local news, we can be ready to talk, even a little, on any topic.

I approach books in the same way. We don't all have the time to read bestsellers cover to cover, so I often read reviews that are only 300 words instead of 300 pages (no one needs to know our secret). I've never read a book in the *Twilight* series, but because I read the newspaper, talk to friends and watch *Entertainment Tonight*, I realized how much coverage and buzz had been given to this bestseller. Again, I wasn't about to pick up that big book, but instead read a few different reviews so I could discuss it. Rather than of being left out of conversations when the topic of *Twilight* came up, I was able to stay in and actually engage in conversation about the book, the movies, its revenues, critics and fans. Sometimes I have more information than someone who's actually read the book!

I don't know what I did before the Internet! It is a great tool of endless information and easy "ink free" access to all the newspapers of the world. But with such unprecedented access to news comes the risk of information overload. When I first started at the Fox News Channel as a political analyst appearing on *The O'Reilly Factor, Fox and Friends, Hannity and Colmes*, etc., I would read for about four hours each morning about everything and everywhere. I'd go online to read the *Washington Post, Washington Times, New York Times, Wall Street Journal, Chicago Tribune, USA Today, Daily Herald, New York Post, LA Times* and *Newsday* among others. I had to sift through each one and figure out what was relevant, pertinent and newsworthy that day, and then stay on top of it once a topic for my segment was selected for the show. Now, many of the broadcast and cable networks' political divisions "edit" down the Internet. They search the Web for the most relevant, news breaking and newsworthy stories of the hour or day and provide a brief synopsis and link to full stories in newspapers around the world. Now, I only read about 90 minutes instead of my previous four hours and this is where I go to get it done:

Politics and Current Events:
cnn.com/ticker
firstread.msnbc.msn.com
blogs.abcnews.com/thenote
thepage.time.com
politicalwire.com
huffingtonpost.com
thedailybeast.com
drudgereport.com

World
alertnet.org
news.bbc.co.uk

Sports
espn.go.com
si.com

Business
bloomberg.com
finance.yahoo.com

Entertainment
eonline.com
ew.com

Pop Culture and Gossip
nypost.com/pagesix
tmz.com

Books
nytimes.com/pages/books

Everything
news.google.com
news.yahoo.com
USAtoday.com
twitter.com

Most of the websites also have areas for you to register for e-mail alerts, daily or as news breaks. This can be especially helpful when you get information on your way to an event that you can announce when you arrive. Not only are you able to impress those around you but most importantly you empower them with information.

Many of us love to listen to music as we get ready for an event, or have a rerun of *Seinfeld* playing in the background. I had two televisions in my White House office and, to be honest, one was often on *Seinfeld* while the other was tuned to CNN. But before any event I would change Seinfeld to CSPAN, so if the President asked me about anything, I could either have an answer or at least be familiar with what he was talking about so I could find the answer! I never, ever wanted to be in a position where I said "I don't know!" or appeared uninformed. If I was asked about a vote on the Hill or breaking news, I was ready for it and you should be, too.

I recommend you take the 30 minutes as you're getting ready to tune in to a TV news channel or National Public Radio (NPR). Check Twitter on the way to the event–it's a great quick-hit place to keep on news events, see what's trending or check your client's most recent post. You'll be amazed at the information you retain that you hear in the background. And always take the time to find out the closing stock positions of any companies that will be present at the gathering before you walk out the door. A stock's performance can tell you when to congratulate and when to just talk about something else!

THE BOTTOM LINE

Whether you are starting a conversation or walking into one in progress, your "Power of Knowledge" will always prevail and leave a smart impression in any situation! Know a little about a lot. It works! It's impressive!

◆ THE POWER OF YOUR APPEARANCE ◆

It is no secret that your first and most lasting impression takes place before you even open your mouth. As exciting and interesting as you may be, some people will forget what you said and remember only what you were wearing! And you certainly don't want all that research and knowledge to go to waste! The good news is you have the ability to control your appearance. But the Power of Appearance is not limited to how you look, which I refer to as the "physical," but it also includes how you carry yourself, which I refer to as the "emotional." Mastering these two factors will determine if you surface and rise out of the sea of guests or if you sink to the bottom (or should we say revert to the lonely corner of the room).

The Power of Your Emotional Appearance

Our knowledge won't shine and what we have to say will not be heard if no one wants to be around us! How do *you* present *yourself?* Do you appear happy or sad, confident or sheepish, approachable or standoffish? Your emotional appearance plays an important role in determining your power as a guest because it sets not only *your* tone but also the tone of the people around you.

Let me tell you about a former White House colleague of mine who had the emotional appearance of a dead man walking. No matter what, he wasn't happy. When there was something for him to celebrate, he didn't want to crack a smile. When people asked him how he was, he would say with a heavy sigh, "OK." You would be genuinely concerned if you didn't know that this was his normal, personal demeanor. Yes, he was good at his job but it was his attitude; you just did not want to be around him. Every Monday I would ask how his weekend was and the response was always the same: "I went out ...didn't meet anyone ...I never do." Well, here's a news flash: If you are pleasant to be around, people will want to be around you. If you are not, people are going to stay away – and when it comes time for that promotion or new account, it is going to be given to someone else.

Don't get me wrong; I am sensitive to and aware of the varying degrees of clinical depression. It can be a serious medical condition and should be treated by a qualified doctor or therapist. So if you have symptoms of medical depression, get medical help. If you are just plain negative, search a few aisles further for Dr. Phil.

How do you respond when someone asks, "How are you?" Great? Good? OK? Miserable? I realize we are not happy all the time, but when "working" the scene, do your best to put away whatever may be bothering you. You're at an event to have fun and further your career. Why act like you'd rather not be there? Producing a positive attitude at an event will put you on the path to obtaining a positive response...and result.

In addition to appearing emotionally positive, you should at least appear emotionally *interested* and pay attention – even if the individual or topic is not your favorite. Another colleague of mine always had a way of making you feel she was doing you a favor by taking the time to talk with you. She appeared maybe one-third into what you were saying; the other two-thirds of her was looking around for someone else to talk to, and eying your hair. Yeah, I know I've had some bad hair days but that can really shake your confidence. Remember, you may not be interested in the topic or person right away but give them a chance, give them your interest. Within a few minutes you may think they are actually the most interesting person in the room! You never know what you could do for them, who they know or what they will need in the future. Five minutes of feigning interest can only help you.

What about confidence and approachability? These are both positive traits and emotions. They can speak to your credibility and self-confidence in what you want to become both professionally and personally. But, these two factors can cancel themselves out. We can all think of someone we know who stands *so* erect as to appear as if he or she has to look down onto everyone else, or someone so full of themselves that they are unapproachable as if to say "Don't talk to me; if *I* want,

I'll talk to you." I can't stand those people, but we all have to tolerate them to some extent. When in a conversation with someone who is so self-obsessed and overconfident that they actually believe they can cross the street without looking – grin, get through it and move on. Minimize your time and remember that overconfidence does not always equal overachiever.

I believe whatever you do and wherever you go, a large part of your success is in how you "carry" yourself. By that, I mean stand up straight, self-assured and confident. Smile and appear approachable and open to conversations, taking time to explore the people around you, even if the only reason you are there is because your boss made you attend. Sometimes that may mean laughing, asking questions or just keeping eye contact and listening. Take the time to realize your odds of reaching your goal are better when you have control of your emotional appearance and can arrive at your event with a positive, approachable and confident attitude.

THE BOTTOM LINE

Enjoy the mood you are in—or put on your best mask! Who knows, you may arrive in a bad mood and leave feeling as if you could conquer the world!

The Power of Your Physical Appearance

Billy Crystal's *Saturday Night Live* character Fernando, based on the actor Fernando Lamas, became known for the catchphrase "It is better to look good than to feel good, because if you look good you feel great!" I believe him! When I look good I feel better, smile and am more confident, which directly impacts what I want to accomplish.

We all come in different sexes, shapes, sizes, colors and heights. We have our own styles, whether it is a three-piece suit, khakis and a collared shirt, skirt suits, pantsuits or the love for the color red. Some of us wear our styles well and some of us...not so well. But in the right size, flattering colors, tasteful accessories and appropriate attire, you can look great, be yourself and feel confident no matter what the event or budget.

Attire

What does proper attire mean? It's the difference between denim and silk, a suit and shorts, heels and flats. And it could mean the difference between making a good impression or a bad one. There are an endless number of attire classifications including casual, business casual, business, cocktail, black tie, white tie, creative black tie and more. Some of these labels may be confusing, and I admit I have added to the confusion at some of my own events.

In 2001, I produced a large St. Patrick's Day/Tenth Anniversary Party for Tom Sheridan, a well respected guy who's 100 percent Irish, and his successful company, The Sheridan Group. It was a lavish gathering of clients, colleagues, friends and family. Except for the setting, which was the elegant

Russian Trade Representation Building in Washington, D.C., the entire event – from the brands of whiskey to the flowers, dancers and music – was truly Irish. When I was planning the event I had a long discussion with Tom about what kind of attire was appropriate for this special Friday evening celebration. We found ourselves choosing between cocktail and black tie but thought neither attire was just right: cocktail was too informal because of the magnitude of the celebration, and black tie was too stuffy for the feel we wanted for the evening. So, we settled on "Creative Green Tie." That night, attire ran the gamut and then some. Men chose tuxedos and suits, green ties and plaid. Some wore green cummerbunds, and there was even a kilt. Women were creative by choosing celadon (green) gowns or adding a silk or chemise green wrap to their dresses. Two guests even wore feathered green boas around their necks and looked…smashing.

I'll admit this was both fun and confusing for the guests. When people called to R.S.V.P., many inquired about the attire and I was able to give a range of ideas and suggestions based on what Tom and his staff were wearing.

The attire can be listed on the invite or expressed verbally by the host. When picking out your wardrobe, take into consideration your surroundings, time of day and day of the week. Picnics are obviously casual and evening gatherings during the workweek are usually business attire. Weekend events can be tricky. They can often be black tie or cocktail attire, so always confirm the dress code at the time of your R.S.V.P. and take time to plan your look *before* the day of the event. Dressing appropriately allows you to fit in while still standing out!

Here are some notes to keep in mind when selecting your attire:

Purpose

Be aware of the event's purpose. Is it a fraternity mixer or a client dinner? Figure it out before the day and dress for it. A friend of mine once showed up for a work meeting in a cocktail dress. She thought the "evening business meeting," where she heard there would be drinks and food, would be more like cocktails and a nice dinner. She put on a cute black cocktail dress after work, went to the restaurant and was directed to the back room. As she walked in she saw a few buckets of beer, sandwiches and desserts (to keep up everyone's sugar levels) with a couple of laptops and white boards to work on a project deadline. There is not much you can do about that awkward feeling after you walk through the door, so don't let it get that far. Clearly understand the purpose and requested attire of the evening and then dress appropriately to forgo any embarrassment.

Your Personal Style

Your personal style communicates how much you care about your appearance and how professional or casual you consider yourself. Your style can reveal whether you are a part of today's technological age and modern world or still believe in yesterday's typewriter.

Personal style can set you apart from the sometimes frumpy or dowdy crowds in your personal and professional scenes. But beware of being too trendy, unless that's your business, and think before you buy.

Get a few staples that are timeless classics and then add something of your own to personalize it and create your own successful look.

Let Someone Else Do the Shopping

Whether you enjoy shopping or hate it, a time-saving option is to make an appointment with a personal shopper at a good department store. Neiman Marcus, Macy's and Bloomingdale's all offer this as a free service. They'll get a feel for what you like to wear, complementary colors and specific events you need to attend. Then they'll let you know the latest trends and standbys, get some ideas and pull them together before you even arrive. You can skip the overwhelming racks of beautiful clothes and go straight to the dressing room, where your properly sized outfits are already waiting! It's a win-win for both you and the store!

Size Matters

No matter what your size, if it fits…wear it. Believe it or not, you will look smaller in something that fits rather than something that is too small or too big. Take your time trying things on; look at the fit in the mirror, not the size on the tag. Don't let the tag discourage you from buying a great outfit! If you have to, take a marker and change the size when you get home!

You're a Shoe-In

I love every shape, height, color and style of shoe. I have more than I need and I have cried more than my share of tears over the pain my feet have endured because of them. But you can find shoes that are both stylish and comfortable. Look for Cole Haan, which integrated Nike technology into its line, or the great collection by Taryn Rose. These are a little pricey but look incredible and feel comfortable. If you can't afford comfort but want to wear some fun styles, invest in a $4 pack of moleskin at your local drug store. It is a second skin you cut and adhere to any blister (or where one is bound to form). Moleskin was a great invention. Take note and buy stock in that!

The Eyes Have It!

Even in the age of Lasik eye surgery and contacts in all colors, many of us still wear eyeglasses. Lucky for us, fashionable frames now make it easy to find a pair we like.

Eyeglasses, even for those who don't need them, have found their place in fashion and functionality. I have a 28-year-old friend who looks like he's 19. He is in broadcast journalism and realized right away that his youthful look worked against him when being evaluated for on-air reporter jobs. So he purchased a pair of great frames with clear glass lenses. He is taken more seriously than before, and is now a successful reporter on *CBS Sunday Morning*. He's not the only one wearing glasses without a prescription. This just proves the power your appearance has on how people judge your talents.

Accessorize With Care

A beautiful necklace can make the outfit and a lapel pin can make a statement. Decide what statement you want to make and then find it in your jewelry box or go shopping! And remember, less is more. You're not Mr. T and a hair scrunchie is not a bracelet!

Hair and Makeup

I love my stylist and you, too, should find one you love! With the right stylist who can frame your face instead of cover it up, and a great makeup specialist who can highlight the natural beauty and lines of your face, you'll be ready to walk through the door! Just remember to let the makeup enhance what you have; don't put on a mask!

Do A 180°

Life is not one-dimensional. So why don't we always turn around and look in the mirror when we try something on. Let's face it, some of us don't want to see our backside, but we have to be strong. Just because we don't see it walking into a party doesn't mean nobody else will. And repeat this in every restroom. I once saw a woman walk through a crowded hotel lobby with her skirt tucked into the back of her nylons. She should have done the 180° but by the time she noticed...it was too late to stop the laughter. That is why you need to turn around and check out all angles before leaving for any event.

THE BOTTOM LINE

Keeping up appearances is not just about showing up. It's about showing up looking and feeling great!

◆ THE POWER OF A GOAL ◆

Whether at our desk or in our homes, almost everyday we write down a list of goals we would like to accomplish. But have you ever done this before going to a social event? Our daily goals may include a list of calls to return, chores to complete or groceries to buy. We carry out these tasks at our desks, in our homes or at the store. But what about social or career goals like impressing a boss for a promotion, finding a new client or a potential donor for a charity? We need to start using social events to meet our goals outside our offices and homes.

You can move yourself off the passive list and on to the active list of guests at a party the moment you choose to set a goal for the event. Passive guests view attending a function as a way to get out of work early, enjoy friends and fill up on the free food. Active guests have the ability to do all of that while achieving their goals at the same time.

I look at setting a goal like creating an agenda. You never go into a business meeting without one, so why would you go to a social event empty handed? You don't have to be in a boardroom to complete a goal. Think about it this way: If you and your colleagues assembled for a meeting every day to make small talk and exchange niceties, what would be accomplished? But when you start each meeting with a list of goals, you achieve them.

In a business meeting, we check off items on the agenda, or "to do" list, as we go along. Attending an event is no different. Whether you are looking to start a relationship with someone you meet at a charity event, a baseball game or the gym, your goals will be easier to achieve if you think of them before you attend. Write them down and then come home and check them off!

In fact, I love checking things off of my to do list! If I do something that was not on my list, I write it down just so I can check it off! Take a moment after you do your research and write down one or two goals – even as simple as "collecting five business cards tonight." Now that you have goals for an event, you will be more likely to achieve them and be productive. If you do not take the time to set goals, your research, knowledge and appearance will all be for nothing.

So think about what it is that you hope to accomplish at your next social event. Is your goal to find a new job? Get a promotion at work? Increase your personal or professional notoriety in your community? Find a new member for your professional or service organization? Whatever your goal, realize that nothing is out of your reach at an event!

THE BOTTOM LINE

No goal is too big or too small when attending a
social event. Set one for your next event and you'll
see how five minutes of thought before you arrive
can produce long-term results.

◆ THE POWER OF YOUR ◆ BUSINESS CARD

Did you know Japanese culture views a business card
as an extension of a person? When I was preparing to meet
someone with the Japanese delegation to discuss an upcoming
State Dinner at the White House, I received my usual briefing
from the State Department's Office of Protocol. Among other
customs and traditions they pointed out, it was noted that
when a member of the delegation hands you his business
card, you are to treat the card with respect as if it is truly an
extension of himself. When offered a card, you should receive
it with both hands, your index and thumb on the two bottom
corners. Instead of immediately putting it away into a folder or
your pocket, you are to keep it in your hands and refer to it in
conversation to show respect.

That lesson really taught me the power of the business
card. The card itself may be just a piece of paper with information
on it, but when it is given to someone it becomes an extension

of you. It has value, it has an emotion. And that impression or emotion you tag it with will determine if the person you gave it to throws it away, keeps it on their desk or enters your information into their contacts!

Since your business card is an extension of you – what do you want it to say and how do you want it to look? One of the best parts about the White House was the embossed business card. A gold raised seal of the President was centered and set the tone. My name and title was below with simply The White House written on the lower left and my telephone on the lower right. I can no longer use the seal or address, but the White House style taught me to display information in a way that is easy to understand, yet stands out from all the rest. These are my tips for when you design your card:

Stock

Use heavy paper stock so that its texture separates yours from all the rest.

Shape and Layout

Be creative with the shape and layout of your card. You can create a square card or one that is slightly larger or narrower than the rest. You can print it horizontally or vertically for something different that stands out.

Colors

Your business card is an extension of your brand, and every good brand uses color in its messaging. Use the colors on your logo or your website on your business card. If you haven't established a color palette yet, combine two that call attention and complement each other, such as orange and grey. Stay away from the basic black that everyone else is wearing.

Fonts and Letter Sizes

More than two fonts on a business card can be confusing. I like using the largest font for your name, title or business with slightly smaller lettering for the particulars.

Information

Keep your information concise. I do this by using E: before my e-mail address and T: before my telephone number to keep the card uncluttered.

Logos and Pictures

Use a picture or logo that identifies you. I have my picture in a small box centered at the top so those who receive it can place my name with my face even weeks after we've met.

Don't Waste Space

Use the back! You're buying that piece of paper anyway and to use the opposite side is a nominal charge. The back of mine is the cover of my book for easy association to remind the person what I'm about.

Keep It Current!

No one likes to explain why they had to cross out their phone number and hand-write a new one in. Did you lose your job? Are you a bad proofreader? Too lazy or cheap to order new ones? There are many online resources like VistaPrint.com or NextDayFlyers.com that specialize in low-cost business cards and can turn them around within 24 hours! There's no excuse not to keep yours current.

Keep Your Cards Handy!

Know where your business cards are at all times! Don't leave them in your desk, hotel room or house! Take them with you – add them to your checklist along with your keys! Cards can be the keys to some opportunity doors! Make sure they are *easily* accessible. I have an embarrassing story of my own that always reminds me to have them ready. In 2002, I was keynoting a dinner in New York City. Afterward the hosts invited me for a drink at the hotel bar. As the night was winding down and folks were heading up to their rooms and I was about to as well, a gentleman I had been speaking to over cocktails asked for my business card. I reached into my pocket feeling what I thought was my card and instead took out and handed him...my room key! OK, way different signal than I wanted to send! Since then, I always keep my business cards in one pocket and in another pocket keep my room key, cash and business cards I receive from others. You only have to do something like that once to remember to always have your cards accessible!

Don't Be Shy

Make your cards available to anyone with whom you're speaking. Give them away like water. On the whole they are actually really cheap compared to all the other ways you spend money on yourself and your business. No matter your level of interest in someone you have met (unless you don't want them to know where you work or live), give out your cards to anyone who asks or you encounter!

Variety

When I am on a speaking tour, the card I hand to participants and potential clients has detailed information on the back about my seminars. When I am out at a cocktail party in the city, I have a streamlined card that highlights my book title and lists me as a lecturer, author and commentator, but I refrain from listing specific seminar titles. That would be done verbally and as a next step.

In this age of side jobs and multiple responsibilities, I believe in multiple cards. If you have a side business, have a card for that as well as your "day" job. If you are heavily involved with a nonprofit organization on whose behalf you attend events that deal with similar issues or sponsors, make up a card for that, too. College and even high school students or unemployed "freelancers" should have a card that can say "freelance" or "consultant." Never give someone the excuse of not having your information as a reason not to call.

THE BOTTOM LINE

You have the opportunity to go home with every person you meet via your business card. If you've communicated the right message of yourself at the event, your business card will keep communicating that message when that person empties his or her pockets the next day or sees the card sitting on his desk. That card is a tool, a reminder of who you are, what you do and how you do it!

THE POWER OF ◆ AN INTRODUCTION

Now is your one chance at your first impression, so make every introduction count! You are already looking good and in a positive frame of mind from your Power of Appearance. You've done your research and have the baseline of knowledge for any conversation, but you kick it all off with...the introduction!

Introductory Lines

A clean slate and a head start! Through your Power of Research you already know who is likely to be there and you've determined whom you want to meet. You also should have some idea of what you'd like to say when that meeting happens. I am not talking about an elevator speech, rather just an introduction. It may sound plain and simple, but I look at it as easy and comfortable. By introducing yourself and not immediately presenting your entire resume and life's history, no one instantly thinks the other person wants something or is identified with something negative. If you keep it plain and simple you can start building a relationship that may eventually lead to a mutually beneficial partnership.

What's Your Line?

You know you will be introducing yourself to someone you've never met. So why not prepare your line and think about what you will say before you say it? What you say often depends on where you are. For example, are you going to a professional industry event where it is appropriate to identify yourself with your business title? Are you at a fundraising dinner where you should identify yourself as being dedicated to the cause of the evening? Or are you simply a parent enjoying your kid's soccer game? By looking at where you will be, what you'll be doing and why you are there, you can find a commonality with the person you are meeting. Your foundation to a new relationship can be based on a **common bond** that brought you both to the event. That may be baseball or school if you're at your kid's game, it could be spin class if you're at the gym, it could be a business if you're at a conference. It may be a specific charity, or politician if you're among thousands cheering at a rally. Find that bond ahead of time and be prepared to use it.

Some of us are comfortable striking up a conversation with someone we've never met. However, some of us need more than a name to go off of to start an introductory conversation. Use the background you've researched on the event and possible guests to form a **question** to initiate conversation beyond the introduction and eventually get to what they do professionally. A question allows you to gather information about the other person. By listening to the response, you can create a nice discussion with a follow-up question that can lead both of you to what you do and, most importantly, what you can do for each other. The formula starts to take shape: A **Greeting** through a **Common Bond** plus a relevant and friendly **Question** leads to **Information** about the individual that you can use to create a discussion and foundation for **Relationship Building** to see what **Bridges** they can build for you or you for them, which may lead to a **Partnership.** The relationship building and eventual partnership may take place at a second meeting (lunch or run in at the next event) but this initial introduction lays the foundation of a possible partnership or just great friendship!

The Power of Being Introduced By Someone Else

Being introduced to someone you want to meet by a friend or colleague is a great way to establish credibility. As long as you know your colleague or friend is in good standing with the person you want to meet, this is an excellent way to make contact. Think of it as being set up on a date – you trust the friend that set you up so you'll invest at least a short conversation on a chance to see what evolves, whether that's into a meeting, first date or partnership. It's always nice having someone establish the groundwork for you!

The Power of Introducing Someone Else

Introducing someone to another acquaintance of yours who you feel would be mutually beneficial can really boost your credibility. Connect someone you know to someone else who you know; it's all about being the "B". "A" can't get to "C" without the "B". You're pivotal! People who can bring people together always impress others. It's worthwhile being the "B". When you introduce two people to each other for the first time, say their names clearly to each other and then add a line on what each one is involved in for fun or what they do for a living – whatever it is that you already know they have in common. You can get the ball rolling because they may find something they can potentially do for each other. Your introduction can lead to a relationship or partnership that could enhance or even change their lives!

THE BOTTOM LINE

Introduction Formula:
Greeting + Common Bond + Question➡Information
= Relationship Building ➡Bridges

◆ THE POWER OF A DATE ◆

Sometimes attending an event with a guest has a real advantage, especially when they can introduce you to someone you've been wanting to meet. But in other scenarios it can be a hindrance or even inappropriate. I have a few tips when it comes to choosing or not choosing a date to accompany you to an event.

Plus One or Plus None?

Is the invitation for you and a guest? The last thing you want to do to your host is to R.S.V.P. for an additional guest when you weren't asked to bring one. So if there is any confusion, call up and ask the event planner or host. You'll save yourself the embarrassment by knowing the status ahead of time.

Role Playing

Based on your goal for the event, a date could help you or hurt you. Different events can call for different, shall I say, wingmen? (And yes, sisters or BFFs make excellent wingmen.) If it is a business event and you want to be introduced to some potential clients, a friend or colleague with background and familiarity with the guests may be a good choice to help initiate introductions and conversations. Perhaps you have a friend or significant other who is always great at having fun and attending events and, at the same time, can understand what you need to get done, as well. You may need to explain to your date, who hopefully will understand, that you want to attend the event to meet new people, not hide in the corner and make out. I've dated some great guys who get it and can hold a conversation with anyone and not require the hand-holding others seem to need. Other guys I've dated can't understand why, for two short hours while we are at a cocktail party, he is not the center of attention. You really need to figure out what role you will have and that of your guest based on the goals you want to achieve. Then you can check "plus one" and make it a great evening!

☑ THE POWER OF A CHECKLIST ☑

Before you leave for any event, don't leave without:

☐ **Confirming**

Whether a phone call or e-mail to the host confirming your attendance, a "Looking forward to seeing you" (maybe even a note to a few other perspective guests) will be appreciated. You can go out of your way where others won't. You begin making an impression before you even arrive!

☐ The Briefing Book

Take out your research notes and refresh yourself before you leave or while on your way to the event. You spent the time putting the plays together, now try them out on the field.

☐ Knowledge

Take a quick look for any late-breaking news on the Internet and check the close of the markets or latest stock quote for a company you may encounter if applicable. Turn off the music and turn on the news so you can get current on the events of the day.

☐ Invitation

You may have to show it at the door.

☐ Identification

Depending where you are going and how high the profile of the event – you may need to show ID to get in, whether for security or to pick up your ticket.

☐ Cash

Don't forget to stop at the cash machine (asking to borrow is so high school). Always have cash on hand. You never know when the open bar turns out to be a cash bar.

☐ Credit Card

I never leave home without it! Besides, if you are buying your ticket at the door, it's easier to keep track of tax write-offs using a card rather than cash. I get miles on my favorite airline when I use mine, so you might as well charge it!

☐Cell Phone

Bring your cell phone, especially if you find yourself running late or hitting traffic. Call when you know you're going to be late and you'll be excused – no note needed. Make sure your cell's charged before walking out of your house or office and have the numbers of the event/taxi services, etc., with you. Most importantly, turn the phone off when you arrive at the event. If you are expecting a very important call, turn it to vibrate and when it signals, excuse yourself to check the number and have the conversation.

☐Important Numbers

Bring contact information for the host, your guest if applicable, the location and a list of taxi services if needed following the event.

☐Mints

<u>Never</u> leave home without these either. Make them sugar free; sugared mints can compound the problem you already have!

☐Business Cards

Whether it's a new business prospect or a possible date for Saturday night, you want them to have your contact information. Always have enough cards along and make sure they are accessible. It looks so sloppy when you have to search the bottom of your briefcase or purse to find one or, worse yet, pull out your city bus card by mistake!

☐**Pen and Paper**

You never know when you'll want to make a note about a conversation while it's fresh in your mind.

☐**Host Gift**

If the event is at the host's home or a special, private location somewhere, bring something for them. A bottle of medium-priced wine is always a great standby or, better yet, something they collect or are interested in will really score you some points!

☐**Incidentals**

Lipstick, powder, perfume, deodorant spray, contact case.

RIGHT BEFORE YOU LEAVE ...

☐**Lips and powder!**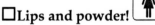

A nice lip color will make you feel brand new and taking that shine away will give you a finished look.

☐**Shirt and Razor!**

A clean shirt after a long day is always a must – you'll feel the difference and everyone else will see it. Don't be afraid to take out your charged razor from the desk drawer or the glove compartment to give you a fresh and confident look.

☐**The Quick Fix**

Grab something like a power bar or even crackers from the vending machine and have something to eat before you leave or while you're on the way. Why? Won't there be plenty of food at the party? Probably, but why would you want to stand around the buffet eating all night when you could be meeting people and grabbing new accounts instead of Swedish meatballs? Besides, it's hard to carry a plate in one hand, a drink in the other and attempt to shake hands. So eat a little something first; the alcohol won't go to your head and you can keep eye contact with the person you're talking to instead of on the buffet as you wait for them to refill the mini beef sandwiches. It's always easiest to take from the passed hors d'oeuvres – this way no plate – and you're left with only a napkin you can stuff in a pocket!

That's it! You're ready! It's Showtime!

SHOWTIME

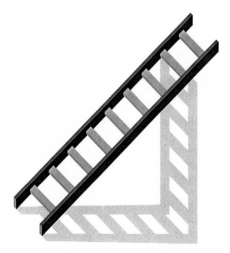

WE'VE ALL BEEN TO A PLAY where the curtain slowly opens for the first act, or we've watched the beginning of a movie scene where someone snaps down the scene marker and the director yells "Action!" It's Showtime. This is where it all comes together. The actors have rehearsed for this moment. They've memorized their lines. They've been to wardrobe and makeup, and now are ready to hit their marks. Attending an event is your "Showtime." Now is the time to hit *your* mark. Again, you have only one chance to make your first impression, and you're ready! You've done your research and preparation. You've learned the back stories of important people who will be in attendance. You know how this scene can unfold and come together. By making that first impression strong and positive, it will not be soon forgotten.

◆ THE POWER OF TIMING ◆

Whoever created the phrase "fashionably late" was just plain late. Can you imagine an actor being late, leaving the audience in silence after the curtain opens? We all know timing is everything. Although I don't encourage you to get to an event "early," I do recommend you get there right on time - within five to 10 minutes of the invitation time. If you're late you miss the opportunity to talk with people before it gets so busy that they are pulled in multiple directions – away from you. It also makes it easier to meet guests as they arrive. Instead of you having to find someone to talk to when you come in, be the person other people look for when they first arrive: a friendly and inviting face. This is your chance for an easy audience and a perfect opportunity for you to put all that research to use.

Is there such a thing as too early or too late? No host likes it when the first guest is pulling up in the driveway and they have to answer the door with wet hair. If you're early, hang back in the lobby or stop short of the location and grab a coffee until invitation time. If you're going to arrive 30 minutes or more after invitation time, you are considered officially late and risk offending the host and other guests! Don't make your host feel as if he or she was second or third on your list of priorities for that day or evening. In all cases be smart and call ahead if you are running very late. If you know you have another earlier engagement, let the host and a few other guests know to spread the word that you have a prior commitment but will be arriving as soon as possible – because, of course, you wouldn't want to miss it! Take it from someone whose roots are in politics: You can spin anything!

Your departure is as important as your arrival. No matter how much fun you are having, if it is an hour or even 30 minutes past the suggested end time, take your signals from the host, who at that point may want to hand you a broom to start cleaning up! Don't be a hanger-on or that one lonely guy who is known for staying too long. Think of it like Steve Carell's decision to leave *The Office*; leave when you're still on top, not when your ratings take a dive.

No matter how you're arriving or departing, your mode of transportation plays a role. Always remember to schedule your departure for an on-time arrival and a smooth exit. Consider your options in advance:

If it's public transit...

Find the closest subway, bus or train stop and make sure you know when the last one leaves the station. If I take a subway to the event and its location is near my stop, well lit and familiar, I'll take it home. When the station is not close or well lit, I'll have the numbers to some taxi companies and choose that for my departure. Whether the cab ride is all the way home or a five-block trip to the train stop, it is *always* safety first and worth the fare!

If it's a taxi...

Have the event address on hand so you can tell the driver right away and carry phone numbers to two or three taxi companies. Better yet, if your city has a mobile taxi service such as Uber or Hailo, be sure to have their apps downloaded onto your phone and your account information on file. It can be a lifesaver when you're trying to leave a party in a location that doesn't see a lot of cab traffic.

If it's a private car...

Get the cell number of your driver before you get out of the car at an event and give an approximate time you'll want to depart. This way, about 10 minutes before you leave, you can call the car to the pick-up area. This is important in case the driver decides to catch a bite to eat or falls asleep.

If it's your own car...

If you have an option to valet – take it! You'll look better, it's not going to break the bank and, besides, if it's business, you can write it off. If valet parking isn't an option, find a spot as close to the door as possible. Remember, safety first! It's going to be dark when you leave later, so look at your surroundings and get familiar with them. If this place is sort of out of the way, dark and unfamiliar, ask someone to walk you to your car. Just remember to play it smart; most of this seems like common sense, but it's amazing how after one drink we can forget it all!

If it's a shuttle...

Sit next to someone new! What a terrific opportunity to start a conversation before you arrive at your destination. You may make your best contact before you even get to the event!

THE BOTTOM LINE

Whoever said timing is everything...was right!

◆ THE POWER OF LISTENING ◆

Larry King once said, "I never learned anything while I was talking" and he is right. Listening is a powerful tool to gather information. It is an opportunity for you to realize what bridges you could build for the person you are speaking with or where they have bridges in their social diagrams you may need to access. A conversation that starts out slow could end up being fascinating, not to mention beneficial. You never know what you can do for them, who they may know or what they will need in the future. Stick with it: Five minutes of feigning interest may lead to the best conversation of the night!

THE BOTTOM LINE

It's better to impress someone by showing interest in them than to talk too much about yourself. During these one-sided conversations, seek out a common interest or subject you want to discuss.

◆ THE POWER OF CONVERSATION ◆

A formal dialogue, chit chat, *tête-à-tête*, huddle, catch up, discussion, exchange of ideas; no matter how you say it, when you're saying something, it's a conversation and it's powerful.

Without question, the most precious commodity we have is

time. Time to do the things we love with people who bring value into our lives professionally and personally. In fact, you could say conversation is a gift to exchange with someone else. Whether a hello and smile to the mailman as you walk by, a friendly exchange with a stranger as you ride in the elevator, instructing your colleagues about a task at hand, meeting someone at a bar or even discussing life late into the night… everything is a conversation, but there are no "do-overs" in conversation.

If you want to make an impression with someone you just met or someone you have wanted to meet, make it count. Your advance work in the Power of Knowledge, Research and Introduction have gotten you to this point. You are ready to have a great conversation, one that may last just a few moments or continue for the rest of your life.

Take Your Cue

As I have stated, the fine line between business and pleasure is gone, but when it comes to conversation there are two types of general topics. I call them "cocktail" and "business." If the event is strictly business like a board meeting, conference or retreat – conversation leads with that: business. What's new with the company? How are current events affecting what you do? Is there a specific client or project you want to pursue? Cocktail-driven conversation tends to be casual and personal, and a more appropriate place to talk about your home life, hobbies and personal stories. You've had these kinds of conversations many times, but once you master the Power of Conversation you can steer the topics, gather information and create opportunities to offer a bridge in your social diagram, or find one to cross in someone else's social scenes.

It may start out as business or cocktail, but at some point whether it's during a break in the daylong seminar or the line at the bar – there will be an opportunity to dig deeper into the conversation. I'm not suggesting you ask someone to lie down as you play therapist, but don't just ask what a person does for a living – find out what he or she *likes* to do. What are they involved in? Thanks to your research and your ability to listen for cues in the conversation, you can navigate toward a topic that's familiar to the person you're talking with, and also interesting for you.

When I first moved back to Chicago after eight years at The White House, I was out with some girlfriends at a favorite neighborhood pub when we met some guys that also lived nearby. When one of them asked me what I did, I responded professionally with "event strategy and communications," and the guy just looked at me and said: "No, I meant like – do you rollerblade or play volleyball at the beach?" It was exactly the conversation I needed to decompress after eight years in Washington. It was a welcome awakening for me in my new life "outside the beltway."

Making Your Move

Looking for a conversation? Are you a party of one looking to meet some new friends or clients? When attending an event, there are some easy signals to read that let you know if the road is open or closed!

Reach outside of your circle, which sometimes may mean

reaching outside your comfort zone. Try sitting next to someone you don't know at dinner, or make a point of talking to five new people at the networking happy hour, using their nametags as a starting point for conversation.

Whether you are starting a conversation or walking into one in progress, the Power of Knowledge will always prevail. Knowing a little about a lot will allow you to participate in any conversation. You never want to be squeezed out just because of the topic. Prove that you can hold your own no matter the conversation, but don't forget to listen! Make a mental note of where your social diagrams may overlap and where you can help each other.

Most importantly, include everyone, regardless of first impressions. You never know if you're speaking with the next Susan Boyle, the surprise star from *Britain's Got Talent*. I learned this lesson from my parents and it was reinforced for me by President Clinton. Through eight years of working the rope line with him after events or walking through crowds, it was always interesting to see President Clinton talk to everyone. Now, we all know he loves to talk, but he literally would stop and talk to anyone, even if they were complaining or not of voting age. He understood he had a responsibility to respect people's questions and concerns no matter if they are Democrat, Republican, Independent or indifferent. Whether they agreed with his policies or not, he would hear them out. He taught me never to count anyone out. You never know what you can learn from the other, who knows who, or how you can be of help to each other until you have a conversation.

The Name Game

Whether you just met someone new or have known this person forever, it is important to use names! For example, did you know if you use a person's name, they are more likely to listen and follow you intently in conversation? By doing so, you make what you say important to them. It makes the other person aware you are listening and interested in what they have to say. Try it and test the response!

Name-dropping is entirely different. People can see right through it. What if they don't like the person whose name you just dropped? Stick with yours and theirs to make an impact! That's what my friend Brad Pitt told me.

If you have to drop someone's name, make sure it's your own, that way, people are more likely to remember it. What if the other person doesn't remember you from a year ago? If it's a loud room, they may not have heard your introduction. It's always safe to repeat your name to reinforce. Here's an example: mutual friend Amy introduces Laura to Meghan:

Amy: "Meghan, I'd like you to meet my friend Laura, she lives in your neighborhood.
Laura: "Laura Schwartz, nice to meet you Meghan."
Meghan: "Great to meet you, Laura."

The person you meet will thank you for it, especially if they had momentarily forgotten your name.

How do you remember people's names? Many people stand by mnemonic devices like rhyming a new name with something you are familiar. As for me, I like to repeat the name upon meeting – that way they can correct me right away if I have it wrong or am mispronouncing it. I also try to associate his or her name with something I can remember. At a recent event, my friend asked me if I recalled someone's name. I said it's Amanda, and the only way I can remember is when I first met her I thought "she could be A MAN, she's so tall." There's a great guy at my gym whose name is Andy and I could never remember it until I connected him with *Toy Story* the movie because he's thin and cute like Woody, the lead character, and the kid's name in the movie was…Andy. So every time I see him I think Woody silently to myself and then say: "Andy! How are you?"

Getting Behind the Wheel

There is no doubt that the most effective way to steer a conversation is through your Power of Research. You should have already prepared bullet points for conversations and have reviewed information on things you know will be of interest to the host and guests, which gives you a head start. I don't look at this as a script but rather an outline to loosely follow – just like Larry David, co-creator of *Seinfeld* and creator of HBO's *Curb Your Enthusiasm*. Larry doesn't write a script for *Curb*, but rather an outline of points he wants the actors to make. The result? Countless Emmys and critical acclaim.

With an outline you are able to ask well-informed questions and encourage open conversation. Play a little Oprah; ask questions and let your guest answer them. But don't confuse your conversation with a hard-hitting interview on *The O'Reilly Factor*, where the guest is often in the hot seat instead of a comfy chair. Confrontation is not conventional conversation and can easily end a chat before you reach your goal. Being a bully at a party can be a real killjoy.

Also, remember people like to believe they are experts on everything. If you are interested in something they are talking about, ask a question. While they are elaborating you can find a way to continue the conversation at hand or find a "lead" into a new topic and create a natural transition into a point you want to make, or a subject you want to discuss. For some pointers just watch any cable news program. Hosts like Bill O'Reilly, Chris Matthews, Wolf Blitzer, Charlie Rose and Sean Hannity are good at what they do because they are active listeners and have an outline in their heads. They know in which direction they want a conversation to go, and have the ability to steer the talk so they get there!

Curtain Call

Just as you watch for the right opportunity to break into a conversation, know when it's time to break it off. Recognize when the person you're talking to is ready to move on. They may have a list of goals they want to accomplish and people they want to meet just like you. Take these cues and you'll be rewarded later. Close the conversation, exchange cards and ask to continue the conversation over lunch or coffee. This will give you credibility, make them feel valuable and give you both a graceful exit and possible second act!

Exit Strategy

There are many getaway routines. If you want the person you came with to bail you out, there are always those predetermined baseball signals (maybe your hand through your hair) to prompt a rescue. But initiating your exit can be as simple as saying, "It's been great to meet you, but I don't want to monopolize your time. Enjoy the rest of your night. I hope we see each other again soon." You could introduce your guest to someone else you know, and let them both continue speaking as you close it out and walk away. You can offer to get the individual a drink; if they say yes, bring it back and politely excuse yourself as if you do not want to intrude on his or her new conversation. Then there's the old standby; excuse yourself to the powder room, wash your hands, pop a mint and come back out to approach your next individual for conversation.

Back to Basics

The simple reality of conversation is that oftentimes people just love to hear themselves talk and they love to talk about themselves – so let them! It's better to impress someone by showing interest than talking too much about yourself. Your opportunity will come; just be patient. That might be tough when the person you've waited all night to talk to is boring you to death with his fly-fishing stories, but don't give up yet! At some point his monologue will culminate with his fish dinner, thus ending the story and providing an opening for you to steer the conversation in a new direction or take that story's closure as an out and move on.

Open Conversation

When your body language does not match what you're saying, one can cancel out the other. Studies have found more than 80 percent of what you say can be interpreted through body language. So it's important to not only be in tune with what you're saying, but how your body is saying it! Always be aware of your arms and don't cross them, lest you send a message that you're not interested or disapproving. And when you smile…really smile! No matter how much you try to pull it off, a fake is a fake, and it's easy to spot. If it's a real smile, your forehead will crinkle and no matter how young you are, crow's feet will form from the corner of your eyes.

Be aware of what other people are saying with their body language. It will indicate if they are done speaking with us or if they are approachable. Identifying common body signals can provide valuable conversation clues.

Last Call

Office jokes the day after a party aren't funny if you can't remember them. Cocktail parties offer great opportunities for successful conversation and connections but they can be dangerous, too. If you're looking to make a good impression, try taking it easy on the alcohol. It's much easier to start off on the right track than to try to shake your reputation as the office lush later.

I am never going to tell you not to drink at an event. In fact, if it will help you relax to have a drink, you should. But keep in mind that although alcohol may make you more talkative, it doesn't make you more informed, interesting or credible. I was recently at an annual event for a women's organization. There were 300 members present and the speaker obviously hit the bar before her speech. Not only were there snickers but guests actually started to drift back into another reception area to speak to each other instead! Know your limits and reduce your chances of exceeding them by making sure you never go out on an empty stomach. You can always ask the bartender to pour your vodka sodas heavy on the soda. They'll last longer and so will you!

Do's and Don'ts

The key to successful communication is remembering the basics. Keep these conversational do's and don'ts in mind at your next event.

Don't Loud Talk

Why are some people just simply not aware of their own volume? Whether they are at home, in the office, at a NASCAR race, in a restaurant or on a train, they have the same volume in every situation. The best way to remedy this is to be aware of your surroundings; no one wants to be screamed at, under any circumstance. If you're a loud talker, recognize it, and practice toning it down.

Don't Over Talk

Isn't it annoying when you're making a point and someone chimes in over you to make their own comment before you finish? Great, then don't do it to others. The easiest way to earn respect is to show respect. Hold your point until you can slot it in at the right time. No one will be annoyed, and you will make a much larger impact on your audience.

Don't be a Topic Tease

This occurs when you switch topics before the last one is completed. It happens when you treat a conversation like sprints on the football field, where you start in the end zone with one topic, run to the 50-yard line with another and all of a sudden you're back at the 10 with the previous topic. This will not win you the Best Conversationalist Award at the annual picnic. Choose your topic, make your point and then move on.

Don't Babble Talk

Not finishing a thought is one thing, but dragging your point out endlessly can be even worse. How many conversations have you been in when the topic just won't die? The subject has been talked out and needs to be put to rest, but the intoxicated colleagues who know a little on the topic have suddenly become experts who need to rehash and repeat everything that's already been said.

Don't Fall into the "Me Too" Syndrome

Although we have all seen others do it, we often fail to recognize when we're mindlessly nodding in agreement just to stay awake and engaged. Slipping into the automatic "me too" response can be easy, especially when we are bored. It is also a way of adding something to the conversation when we either aren't listening or when we are unfamiliar with the subject. And sometimes, it's just a way to ingratiate others in the conversation. If you agree with someone on an issue or topic, increase your credibility by stating *why* rather than just saying, "me too."

Do Embrace Commonality

When you have something in common with another person, this is an easy conversation starter, but it can quickly become the "me too" syndrome if not used properly. Think of how great it was in your first year of college when a senior mentioned his or her hometown and you had once visited there, or knew someone who also grew up there. This gives you a right to chime in and keep the conversation going. It puts you into a much better position than walking into a conversation in progress asking, "What are you talking about?" Remember to keep this one simple; never go overboard – no matter how tempting. Don't claim to know someone you don't because you never know who knows who!

Do Carry Breath Mints

There is no bigger conversation killer than bad breath! Although everyone knows the importance of personal hygiene, no one's immune to the effects of garlic chicken satay or those raw onions in the dinner salad. Always be conscious of your breath. This doesn't mean you have to walk around carrying a pack of Tic Tacs in your pocket so everyone knows where you are at all times because of that jingling sound. Instead opt for Lifesavers; they are easy to carry and discharge. Make sure to grab some before you leave the car, house or office and use when needed. Casually slip your hand into your pocket, grab a mint, and at the appropriate time place it in your mouth. Remember, these are good things to share, so if someone asks you for one, be polite and share the minty goodness. It's called a Lifesaver for a reason! If you are having a conversation with someone who doesn't realize his or her breath is bad, nonchalantly offer them one of your mints as you pop one, as well. Last point: smaller mints and Lifesavers are always the best at events. If you're sucking on a large mint, it may look like a wad of tobacco inside your cheek. And please, no gum chewing.

Do Keep Your Distance

Personal space is another consideration when trying to grab the attention of others. Captivating your audience is not the same as cornering a couple of office mates. Be respectful of everyone's personal space; give yourself at least a foot. Just because you are standing up instead of sitting at a table doesn't mean you or the person you are talking to needs less room. Feel it out and be perceptive.

Do Make Eye Contact

Nothing is worse than when you are trying to have a conversation with someone who is constantly looking around you, but not at you! It's as if they are looking for someone better to talk to and not even trying to be discreet. Worse still is the person who stares at nothing but your hair and clothes, making you feel terribly out of place. Learn from others' annoying habits of conversation and make a note to yourself about the importance of eye contact.

Do Use Your Hands

Hand gestures are great as long as you're not making them through your car window at 70 mph. Hand movement can reinforce your point and peak others' interest. Just be sure not to point. Relax your hands and make open gestures so you don't come off as confrontational.

Do Smile

Look friendly, even if you aren't naturally an outgoing and gregarious person, because more people will be inclined to interact with you. Remember misery invites misery. Don't be a part of the bitter circle because no movers and shakers will want to join.

Don't Fidget

Unless you are in a small room, handcuffed to a table with a bright light overhead, there is no reason to squirm. This includes bouncing your knee, playing with your hair, licking your lips, biting your nails – you get the point. This only makes you appear nervous and sends the wrong signals. Relax and enjoy the event and conversation.

Do Watch Your Language

OK, when have you ever used an Andrew Dice Clay monologue to impress your boss? It is amazing how many people use curse words in the most inappropriate ways. Screen yourself and filter your mouth. If you want to strengthen your statement, do it with substance, not slang. If you have a habit of using off-color or curse words in conversational speech, it just looks like you have a poorly developed vocabulary and know no other way to make a point.

Don't Ask About "$'s and #'s"(Salaries and Ages)

It's just simply inappropriate to inquire about personal salaries. And if you are ever asked to "guess" someone's age, lowball the number. Once I guessed eight years too high and never got beyond that first encounter with someone who could have been very beneficial.

Don't Gossip

So the office gossip has cornered you in the middle of the event. No matter how much you may want to hear the juicy news, do not stay and listen – and do not share any of their gossip to try to impress others! If you really want to hear some gossip, call your friends in the mailroom the next day – they know everything!

Do Smell Fresh

This is just a given. If you have body odor, the least you can do is disguise it. Dab a little perfume or cologne on each wrist, ear and knee – how about under the arm while you're at it! But be careful of the opposite effect. Nobody likes a walking flower and you're not going to get far if your conversation companion has to excuse himself to take an aspirin for his headache or to grab some fresh air on the balcony.

Do Make Sincere Compliments

The color brown never looks good on anyone's nose. You can tell when people are sucking up to you, and you can be sure they can tell when you're sucking up to them, too! Keep it simple. Compliment on the obvious like a new hair style, a beautiful dress or nice tie, but limit compliments to a few and support each with the why. Why do you like that shirt or the venue they chose for the event? If you follow up your compliment with a reason, it's credible. But if all you do is compliment everything, it loses its charm. Remember, less is more sincere and believable!

Don't Tell Bad Jokes

We've all heard them, but they are not always universally humorous and could even be perceived as harassment. There are a few ways to approach these awkward situations. First, you can decline to respond and act as if you really were not listening or interested. Or second, whenever in doubt, look at your boss or someone you trust, let them react first and follow their lead. You are what you laugh at, so take the high road and get out of that conversation.

Don't Be a Know-it-All

Nobody knows it all so don't try to act like you do. (Remember the guy in your class you never liked – yeah, the know-it-all.) Try asking questions instead of flaunting your brilliance. People love to feel like experts and if you start on a level playing field you're more likely to make an impression.

Don't Debate

When it comes to politics, all I can say is know your audience! It's easier to stick to policy and discuss the issues themselves as an "Independent" than to force someone to choose political sides when he or she is just out at an event to have some fun. Leave it to the pundits, not the people you've just met, to argue political points or parties. I've felt like a moving target at many events because of my background in politics and I'm used to that, but I never enjoy having my interesting evening interrupted by someone trying to provoke a political argument.

Don't Pick a Fight

There's a time and place to take a stand, but it's not at your kid's football game, an after-hours office happy hour or the annual Junior League dinner. If you must confront someone, do it in private and away from an event. If you're so solid in your conviction and need to clear the air over something that happened, you don't have to be around other people when you do it. Act like an adult and have the "discussion" where it's not awkward – not only for you, but those around you!

THE BOTTOM LINE

Beware of the powers *and* pitfalls of conversation. Taking time to speak with someone, whether it's your first encounter or after 40 years of living or working together, tells the person "I care. I value what you have to say." And that alone is an impression and contribution to someone else's life and your own. Talk is cheap, but conversation is priceless.

Congratulations! You succeeded and found an exciting event during the Casting Call, then worked hard to prepare during Rehearsals. You worked the room and wowed the crowd on opening night. Does this mean Showtime is over? Nope. Now, like any long-running and successful play, you're going to have...an **Encore!**

ENCORE! ENCORE!

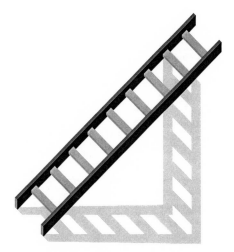

YOU CAN'T STOP NOW! You want to keep that standing ovation going. The show must go on, and your second take can be more powerful than the first. You'll have a chance to critique your performance and showcase yourself even better for the next audience. You're just beginning to understand the Networking Power of Social Events, and as you gain experience and feel more at ease when the curtain rises, Showtime is becoming second nature. You have put so much into attending an event. Now it's time to see it all pay off!

◆ THE POWER OF FOLLOW UP ◆ AND FOLLOW THROUGH

My dad is a big kid at heart. Whenever my sister and I got something cool growing up, Dad wanted to be the first to "show us how it's done." And he always had one phrase he applied to everything. When he taught us how to play baseball, he told us to "follow through" on our swing and "follow through" on the pitch. When we golfed, he always told us to "follow through" with our club; in tennis, it was the same thing with the racket.

When I was about 10, we got this really awesome kite. Eventually, my dad turned it over to me to fly (after testing it out). He told me to start running, so I did. The kite went up and I was so happy that I stopped to watch, and the kite came down. So my dad used that same line again, "follow through." I was like "Dad! That makes no sense. We are flying a kite." But my dad kept at it. He said you've got to "keep running and find the wind; you've got to follow through." Of course, he was right. I had to keep running and keep going. I couldn't just stop once the kite got up in the air; I had to find the right wind to keep it up there.

And that's just what we have to do in life. We get the part, we rehearse, we try to give our best performance, but then we can't forget the encore. We have to *keep going.*

You had a great time at an event and feel like you were on your game. However, you cannot be content with that. All you accomplished, the contacts you made, the relationships you established, the bridges you envision, won't lead anywhere if you don't keep going…and "follow through."

◆ WHAT CONTINUES TO MAKE YOU STAND OUT? ◆

You were a powerful guest. You had interesting conversations, impressed fellow guests with your knowledge about the location, the day's event, the charity and even your fellow guests and their companies. You listened to what people had to say and wanted to share. You offered the use of bridges in your social diagram to others, and you learned what potential bridges exist for you through the people you met and with whom you invested time. You exchanged business cards and have 10 new ones sitting on your desk or kitchen table. Now what? Now is when you solidify the new relationships you've put in motion by following up and following through.

Many people think they are good at follow up. Some believe if they whip off a ton of e-mails from their phone on their way home at 9 p.m. or 1 a.m., it shows the person you just met how much you care. You know what this shows me? You're either e-mailing before you quickly forget because your new contact is not that memorable; you desperately want something; or you're simply going through the motions. And if you are going to whip off a note in the car or subway on your way home, at least take the time to delete the bottom line that says "sent from my iPhone" or "sent wirelessly via Verizon BlackBerry." It's like telling someone they only rank high enough for a text, not an actual phone call.

◆ DUALLY NOTED! ◆

E-mail is easy to write, e-mail is easy to delete. But a handwritten note on nice stationery stays on someone's desk, gets pinned on a board, stuck to the fridge, attached to a project, and it stands out. Since it's an extension of you, it means you stand out!

E-mail is immediate and a good way to start a conversation, especially to make sure you have each other's complete information. It can sum up the night before and talk about some ideas you have that may interest someone based on your shared conversation. You can draft this in the middle of the night or on your way home, but send it the next day. Even if I've already written the e-mail hours before, I first start sending out follow-up e-mail between 8 and 9 a.m. This tells people they were the first thing on your mind. You wanted to start your day by reaching out to them. Plus, they receive your e-mail when they are starting the day refreshed and ready to do business. You're right there on the screen, instead of making a distant, incoming message alert sound at 3 a.m. It's impressive. It shows commitment, good work ethic and a sense of priority. But don't stop there!

A handwritten note is a clincher. I'll never forget how much I hated sitting down to write thank you notes after my confirmation and graduations. But my Mom always made me do it and I was always...thanked for it? I got a present, I said thank you when I opened it, I wrote and sent a thank you, and then the person who gave me the present in the first place thanked me for the thank you note!

Wow, a note really impresses when you take the time to send it when you're 11 years old. And it's even more impressive now at your age in this technological era with the immediacy of the Internet. It tells the prospective friend, colleague, mentor or client that you really do care. You are taking the time to do something few others will do after an event. What a way to stand out from the rest! And when you include something in your handwritten note about your conversation with this person, you tell them "I was listening" and, let's face it, a lot of times you leave a conversation never expecting to hear from someone again.

Following an e-mail with a handwritten note continues what you started the day before at the event. Yesterday was the beginning of a relationship, or the continuation of a relationship with someone you already know. But the correspondence the next day and following week is what will continue to build that relationship. Who knows where it will go?

Maybe you want to connect him to someone in your diagram who can help him achieve his goal. Perhaps you want to recruit her to join your service organization, the chamber of commerce or your committee to get her involved in the community. You may want to continue a conversation from the day before about a potential new market for one of your company's products. Maybe she just talked about a good math tutor who could help your child. No matter the reason, building relationships is the basis to long-lasting friendship and partnerships. You're on your way.

◆ THE TWO-STEP IMPRESSION ◆

E-mail
- ✓Send the next day
- ✓Include your complete information under your signature (in case they misplace your card)
- ✓Reference how you met at the event (so they can place you)
- ✓Reference your conversation (shows you listened!)
- ✓Offer a bridge in your social diagram that could connect him or her, or help him or her reach a goal
- ✓Send a follow-up e-mail introducing him or her to someone who may be of interest, and he/she can take it from there. Be the "B"!

Handwritten note

  Do everything above plus:

  ✓Find an article, picture, book or other information you discussed and include it. (Shows you were listening and took the time for an extra step. When that book lands on their coffee table or their desk, so do you...and you're always there!)

  ✓Give this person an action item. Mention an upcoming event you hope to see her at: the next conference, gala or meeting you have in common. Mention somewhere she can look for you, or an idea for her about something to participate in.

  ✓Close with a future invitation for something low-pressure. This can range from "look forward to lunch at the club soon" or "we should try the new cafe you were talking about" or "you'll have to come over and see the new patio; we'll have a cookout this summer." Think of an appropriate invitation to connect with her in person. Then use it as a way to follow up and set a date the next time you see each other or correspond.

My best note was, of course, not just a note. I met a very interesting woman who I had a great conversation with, during which I found out she needed to find a company that could manufacture a product she wanted to take to the marketplace. I connected her with a friend of mine who was able to work with her at a low cost and they made a great team. I sent her an e-mail the day after we met and then a second e-mail cc:ing my friend to make the introduction. This person is now her business partner. But I didn't stop there. We were both in New York when we met. During the conversation we talked about her children, who hadn't made the trip with her but who loved the M&M characters. She was leaving the next day and unfortunately didn't make it to the M&M's Store in Times Square...but I did. The next day I stopped by the store and picked up two M&M banks. I sent a note with them to her address in San Francisco within the same week. It was a nice thing to do, left a huge impression and now she thinks of me every time her kids deposit another nickel. I don't know what bridge she may have for me to cross someday, but in the meantime, I'll do whatever I can for her and it's nice to know I'm on their minds and I've made a great friend.

◆ KEEPSAKES ◆

Everyone knows I love goodie bags! It's that anticipation; there they are all in a row on the tables as you leave a gala event with nice ribbons and tissue overflowing out of the top. But those aren't the only keepsakes I'm taking home from that event, fundraiser, annual conference or holiday party. I am taking home something more valuable. I am taking home information, new friendships, potential friendships and partnerships. But in order to make them powerful, long lasting and productive, I need to take that information, store it, cross-reference it and have it accessible.

I use the Address Book program that comes standard with the Mac operating system. What isn't standard is the fact that you can customize fields to enter specific information and then be able to spotlight it when you need to find it. Instead of the usual name, title and contact information, I create additional fields to build what I call a "Power Profile." It includes their professional background and career goals, their personal activities, interests and goals, family status, event history of how we've met, places we've seen each other and of course a communication history of correspondence, phone calls and topics discussed.

I basically start building a profile on that person, which I can go back to and reference and cross-reference when I build bridges of benefit for them or someone else. I also copy and paste some of our e-mail correspondence into their profile to reference and jog my memory before an event if I'll be seeing this person.

You can do this any way that's easy for you. Create an index card for each person or just create a Word document file and have an ongoing list of names and information. It's sort of a little black book for life, not just dates. Find the best way to create and keep your records. It makes it easier to stay in touch and remain relevant in someone's life.

◆ BE YOUR OWN CRITIC ◆

After a play or movie, the reviews come in. Don't worry. It's easy to take constructive criticism when it comes from you! So critique yourself. When an event is still fresh in your mind, you need to take a look back at what went well, what could have gone better and what just didn't work at all.

Even when you follow each step in the process to become a powerful guest, there is always room for improvement. So often we get home, throw away the brochure, sift through the goodie bags and go to bed. We wake up the next day, maybe make a few calls with friends that were there and talk about the night before, who was there and what we thought of it. But what about what we thought of our individual performance? Did we meet our goals? Did we run out of business cards? Did we have the right date? Did we spend too much time in one conversation we should have tabled for a lunch or nightcap, and instead missed out on maximizing the guest list?

It's best to "write your review" that day or the next to determine what worked and what didn't, to make you better and more powerful for the next! We can always improve!

For some of us, the Power of the Guest comes naturally. For others, it's not so easy. There are the A-type personalities (outgoing and extroverted) and then there are B-type personalities, (introverted and shy). There are all kinds of categories to classify people socially. Well, I don't subscribe to any of them. We are each our own person and we each have our own unique social scenes and abilities. So I ask you to use what you have and find your comfort level, then add in a few of the tips and techniques through the powers I've outlined and take it to the next level. Take a moment to fill out your own Professional Profile as well! You will be better familiar with yourself and ready for the event and follow up as well!

Look at social events as a way to exercise your power as a guest. Just like fitness exercises, your stretch will start reaching farther, your muscles will take shape and your endurance will grow. The best part of it all? The Power of the Guest always happens through interaction with others. The most intimate thing you can do with another person is spend time getting to know who they are. To me, that's what life is all about.

KEEP CLIMBING

MY SISTER AND I have lunch somewhere together every Sunday. It's our time to talk about what we may have missed from the week before and look forward to the week ahead and events to come. We eat, drink and truly feel like we are ready to succeed, no matter what stresses and barriers we face in the week ahead.

Because whenever, wherever and whatever you eat and drink with someone – you will both be ready to succeed. Whether a power bar and bottle of water with your teammate; a martini and stuffed olives over cocktails; beer and nuts that you shell on the floor at the corner bar; coffee and pastries after church; bloody Mary's and brunch; a seven-course meal at a state dinner; or, a coffee and bagel while sitting with your fellow commuters on the train – you have the power to succeed. You have the power to share your bridges, at every rung of your ladder, with those you know and have yet to meet. And, most importantly, now you know how to use it. So get out there and Eat, Drink and Succeed…it's Showtime!

POWER REFERENCE

Your Check List to Eat, Drink and Succeed!

SETTING THE SCENE
❑Create and continually update your social diagram

CASTING CALL
❑What is the event?
❑Find an event
❑Get Involved
❑Who else is attending/invited?
❑What scenes crossover?
❑R.S.V.P.

DRESS REHEARSAL
One to five days before the event!
❑Assemble The Briefing Book (who, what, when, where, how!)
❑Set and review your goal
❑Send e-mail to the host "looking forward to..."
❑Send e-mails to those you expect to see "looking forward to..."
❑Create talking points for critical conversations
❑Write your "line" and be ready to use it
❑Confirm attire, purchase if needed

Day of!
❑Practice your line
❑Repeat your goal
❑Read the headlines from every section of the paper
❑Log on CNN.com or MSNBC.com to check breaking news
❑Check most recent stock quotes if applicable
❑Re-confirm your attendance
❑Confirm the location
❑Confirm your transportation plan
❑Change shirt/blazer/shoes/outfit – note attire requirements

❑Grab a snack (piece of fruit/meal bar)

❑Shave/make up

❑Pack your bag

    ❑Cash/Credit

    ❑Cell phone

    ❑Pen/notepad

    ❑Mints

    ❑Invitation

    ❑Telephone # of location

    ❑Lipstick/powder

    ❑Contact case

    ❑Single floss pick for teeth

    ❑Brush/comb & mini spray

❑Pack your pocket

    ❑Business cards (accessible)

    ❑Cash/Credit

    ❑Mint

    ❑Small pen

SHOWTIME

Arrival, Event and Departure

    ❑Allow time to arrive on time

    ❑Smile

    ❑Use your introduction and create conversation, watch for body language

    ❑Keep your eye on your goal

    ❑Exchange business cards

    ❑Write notes on business cards while still fresh immediately after the event

ENCORE! ENCORE!

Day After

    ❑Follow up e-mail *and* note to host/hosts

    ❑Follow up e-mail *and* note to current/prospective clients/ relationship possibilities you met

    ❑Review business cards and create/update Power Profiles

    ❑Critique your technique, your introductions, those of others, conversations and build on your performance

POWER PROFILE

INFORMATION PROFILE

Name:
Title:
Company:
Preferred method of contact i.e. office/cell/e-mail/Facebook:
Contacts:
> Office
> Cell
> Pager
> IM
> Fax
> Office mailing address
> Home mailing address
> LinkedIn ID
> Facebook profile name
> Twitter name

Partner's name:
Assistant's name:

PROFESSIONAL PROFILE

Professional goals:
How long in current job:
Prior employment/consulting projects:
Prior cities/locations:
Professional association memberships:
Professional association leadership roles:
Professional association events/dinners/seminars:

ACADEMIC PROFILE

Academic goals:
Undergraduate school/university:
Degree:
Graduate program/school/university:
Degree:
Alumni associations:
Active in alumni association events?
School athletic team, especially if Big Ten:

FAMILY PROFILE

Family goals: i.e. new house/school/location:
Spouse:
      Anniversary date:
      How they met:
Significant other:
      How they met:
Children:
      Names:
      Ages:
      What they are involved in:
      Schools they attend:
      College/universities attend/looking at:
      Jobs they have:
      Where they live:

PERSONAL PROFILE

Personal goals: i.e. marathon, specific travel, community:

Originally from:

Memberships in non-profit organizations:
      Board positions:
      Signature events/fundraisers/runs/campaigns:
Memberships in political/civil action organizations:
      Name of organization:
      Party affiliation if applicable:
      Leadership positions:
      Signature events/fundraisers/campaigns:
Active in community:

Hobbies/Interests:
      Sports: i.e. NFL/National League Baseball
                        City athletics
                        Golf
                        Alumni athletic teams
      Books: Genre
      Concerts: Artists
      Exercise: Gym/Spa membership
      Running: Marathons
      Movies: Genre
                        Favorite actor
      Blogs: List of blogs they participate in
      Food:
      Wine:
      Faith-based organization
            Where attend:
            How active:
            How long:
      Other:

EVENT HISTORY

When did you meet:
Where did you meet:
What was your relationship to the event:
What was their relationship to the event:
Who introduced you:
Who was their date or plus 1:
What topics did you discuss:
Was there anything memorable/interesting/funny that
occurred at the event:
What stands out that you could reference in your follow up:
What bridges did you identify that could help them?
What bridges in their scenes did you identify to help you?
What are future event/meeting opportunities you discussed?

RELATIONSHIP PROFILE

Relationship goals:
>   Become friends:
>   Be the B for A to get to someone you know:
>   Point business their direction:
>   Recruit for membership in your service organization:
>   Recruit for city council/community activities:
>   Assist with their child getting into your alma mater:
>   Introduce to a potential mate:
>   Any goal applies!
>>   List here:

Future opportunities to re-connect:

COMMUNICATION HISTORY

Follow up e-mail:
      Sent date:
      Topic/content:
      Introductions made through e-mail:

Handwritten note:
      Sent date:
      Topic/content:
      Introductions made through note:
      Enclosure in note: i.e. article, gift:

Bridges you offered:
Bridges you discussed:

Social networking site requests/links:
      Facebook:
      Twitter:
      LinkedIn:
      Foursquare:
      Google Plus:
      Pinterest:
      Instagram:

POWER POINTS

SETTING THE SCENE

◆ **What are your social scenes?**

☐ **Inner Circle**
- Spouse
- Life Partner
- Significant other
- Parent
- Sibling
- Close friends
- Close colleagues
- Business partner

☐ **Children**
- PTA
- Sporting events
- Athletic booster club
- Theater performances
- Fundraisers
- Band concerts
- Field trips
- Car pool
- Library reading night
- City athletic leagues
- Moms and tots
- Boy Scouts
- Girls Scouts
- Camps (check out www.kidscamps.com - they list a camp for any interest!)
- Debate
- Forensics
- College prep

☐ **Neighborhood**
- Barbecues
- Football games
- Home renovations
- Birthday parties
- Graduations
- Weddings
- Yard sales

☐ **Faith-Based Organizations**
- Church
- Temple
- Sunday school
- Camps
- Special events and activities
- Retreats
- Seminars
- Board/elder/deacon duties
- Programming
- Greeter/usher
- Volunteering programs

☐ **Service Organizations**
- Lions Club
- Kiwanis Club
- Rotary Club
- American Legion
- VFW
- The Association of Junior Leagues

☐ **Charity and Nonprofit Organizations**
- American Heart Association
- YWCA
- YMCA
- United Way
- Boys and Girls Clubs

- Arthritis Association
- Alzheimer's Association
- Light the Night Walk for Leukemia & Lymphoma
- Meals on Wheels
- Race for a Cure

☐ **Clubs and Leagues**
- Gym/fitness clubs
- Country club
- Recreational pool club
- City athletic leagues
- Private clubs i.e. Union League, University, Metropolitan
- Bowling league
- Book club
- Craft club
- Wine club
- Sports club
- Fantasy football
- Private clubs
- Scrapbooking
- Quilting club

☐ **College**
- Alumni associations
- Colleges
- Universities
- Community colleges
- Master's programs
- Study groups
- Academic organizations
- Greek/independents
- Sports
- College activity boards
- Residence associations
- Honor societies

☐ **Office**
- Client dinners
- Sales conferences
- Annual dinner
- Quarterly meetings
- Happy hour
- Golf outings
- Office picnic
- Coffee breaks
- Baseball games
- Water cooler

☐ **Professional Organizations**
- Industry associations and organizations
- National conventions
- Chapter meetings
- "Networking" events
- Membership associations
- BPW International, International Federation of Business and Professional Women
- BNI, Business Networking International
- Vistage
- Entrepreneurial center
- *Looking for industry associations to join that have local chapters and national meetings for optimal exposure? Check out www.associationexecs.com*

☐ **City and Community**
- Chamber of Commerce
- Community Education
- Concerts in the park
- City arts center
- City sports league
- City historical society
- Fundraisers
- Council meetings

☐ **Political and Civic Action Organizations**
- The Democratic party
- The Republican party
- The Green party
- The Tea party
- Independents
- National Coalition on Family Values
- Mothers Against Drunk Driving
- WIPP, Women Impacting Public Policy
- Greenpeace
- National Coalition for the Homeless
- American Society for the Prevention of Cruelty to Animals

☐ **Social Networking Sites and Blogs**
- Facebook
- LinkedIn
- Twitter
- Google Plus
- Pinterest
- Instagram
- Blogspot
- Gather.com
- Huffingtonpost.com
- Jigsaw
- Spoke
- Plaxo
- Foursquare

◆ **Diagram Your Social Scenes**
➤ List:
  - Your scenes
  - People in your scenes
➤ Create "Power Profiles" for at least two people that you know in each scene.
  - Identify where you can build bridges for others
  - Identify where you can find bridges for yourself
  - Update your diagram anytime you have a new job, position, friend, colleague or social scenes!

CASTING CALL!

☐ **The Power of the Event**
  ► **No event is optional, every event is an opportunity**
  - Business meeting
  - Luncheon
  - Annual convention
  - Charity galas, fundraisers, parties
  - Football games
  - Grand openings
  - Birthday parties
  - Neighborhood picnics
  - Circus

  ► **Get Invited**
  - Use local and national media resources to find a powerful event
  - Look at the news and opportunities bulletins from your school, church, gym, city, etc.
  - Buy a ticket, write it off

  ► **Get Involved**
  - Join a professional/service/charity organization/ club or league
    - Volunteer to help out on the event
    - Access the guest list
    - Earn a free ticket

DRESS REHEARSAL

☐ The Power of Research
- ► **Your Briefing Book**
  - WHO is hosting and attending the event?
    - i.e. company, organization
  - WHAT is the event?
    - Is it a breakfast/lunch or dinner? Business reception or picnic?
  - WHEN is the event and what does that say about the event?
    - Is it in the middle of the day, after hours, a casual atmosphere or business appearance?
  - WHERE is the event taking place?
    - Can you get there? Is it worthwhile to book an airline ticket?
    - Is it conducive to conversation? Is it interesting? Is it familiar?
  - WHY is the event happening?
    - What is the host's goal?
  - HOW can you use the event to build bridges for others and yourself?
    - What is your goal?
    - Will there be crossovers from your social scene? Will there be guests you want to meet who could help you professionally?
    - Is there someone on the board you've wanted to meet?

☐ **Investigate**

► **Using The Charity/Organization's Name**
- Search for the website as well as articles that have been written about it and other companies, groups or individuals that are involved.
- Find where it is based.
- Find out about its director and staff.
- Find who or what companies and groups are active sponsors or partners.
- Research its board of directors, donors, sponsors and frequent guests.

► **Using the Sponsor's Name**
- Search for their website and find out what kind of a business and scenes they are involved in.
- Find what other charities/organizations they sponsor.

► **Using the Co-Chair's Names**
- Search their names using online.
- Find out where they live – local vs. visiting.
- Find any articles that mention them.
- Find out where they/their spouse work.
- Research their business and social scenes.

► **Using the Honoree's Name(s)**
- Same as above: Research like you would a chair/co-chair and be ready to congratulate them.

► **Using the Price of the Event**
- Search or call the organization to find out if they are listed as a 501(c)3 (a nonprofit organization) and what amount of the ticket (if not in its entirety) is tax deductible. To be safe you can always make a quick call to an accountant or ask a friend or boss who attends similar functions how they handle them.

☐ The Power of Knowledge
- Know a little about a lot!
- Headlines from EVERY section.
- Stock quotes, sports stats, book reviews, current events.
- Scan the Web, listen to news live on the Internet/radio before an event.
- Be the one to break the news, not react to it!

► **Knowledge Resources:**
- **Politics and Current Events:**
  www.cnn.com/ticker
  www.firstread.msnbc.msn.com
  www.blogs.abcnews.com/thenote
  www.thepage.time.com
  www.politicalwire.com
  www.huffingtonpost.com
  www.thedailybeast.com
  www.drudgereport.com

- **World**
  www.alertnet.org
  www.news.bbc.co.uk

- **Sports**
  www.espn.go.com
  www.si.com

- **Business**
  www.bloomberg.com
  finance.yahoo.com

- **Entertainment**
  www.eonline.com
  www.ew.com

- **Pop Culture and Gossip**
  www.nypost.com/pagesix
  www.tmz.com

- **Books**
  www.nytimes.com/pages/books

- **Everything**
  http://news.google.com
  http://news.yahoo.com
  www.USAtoday.com
  www.twitter.com

☐ The Power of Your Appearance

► **Emotional**
- Positive Attitude=Positive Response
- Confidence=Credibility
- Approachability=Opportunity

► **Physical**
- Attire: Confirm when you R.S.V.P!
- Personal Style: You are what you wear!
- Size: If it fits wear it!
- Colors: Know them!
- Trend: Invest in the classic, accentuate with trend.
- Shoes: Style + comfort can equal success.
- Eyewear: Use for more than clarity.
- Accessories: Know when too much is too much.
- Hair: Find the style that works on you.
- Makeup: It is not a mask.
- Grooming: Eyes, Ears, Nose, Mouth, Facial Hair, Hands, Upper Body, Legs and Feet.
- 180°: You are not one-dimensional!

☐ The Power of a Goal

➤ Set Your Agenda
  - What do you want to get out of this event? Who are two people you want to meet? How many business cards do you want to give out? Collect? Do you want to prepare a question for the speaker? What bridge do you want to build for someone?

➤ Identify Your Goal Before Attending an Event
  - Just like an agenda for a meeting, if you write it down you're more likely accomplish it!

➤ Record Whether or Not You Met Your Goal
  - Note if you took steps toward that goal.

➤ Sample goals:

New client   Evaluate the location
Promotion   Get 5 new business cards
Access to a play group   Give away 5 business cards
Raise "$" for charity   Find a new vendor
New job   Solidify a contact
New babysitter   Make a friend
Committee position   Try the specialty drink
Political endorsement   See the renovated ballroom
Trustee position   Get a goodie bag
Association membership   See an old friend
Meet the keynote speaker   Verify a rumor
Meet the honoree   Support a friend
Meet the chairperson   Support a cause
Meet the sponsor's CEO   Have a good meal
Meet the event producer

□ The Power of Your Business Card

- Current: Keep information up to date!
- Accessible: Keep them handy!
- Available: Give them out to anyone who asks!
- Stock: Use texture to separate from the rest.
- Shape and Layout: Be creative and sharp.
- Colors: Use colors that stand out.
- Fonts: Two + logo = easy to read and remember.
- Information: Keep it concise.
- Logos and Picture: Use to identify you.
- No Wasted Space: It has two sides, use them both!

□ The Power of an Introduction

- ► Introducing Yourself
  - What's your line?
  - Business/corporate vs. charity/personal.
  - Using your name.
  - Using their name.

- ► Formula

  Greeting + Common Bond + Question
  ➡Information = Relationship Building ➡Bridges

- ► Getting Introduced by Someone Else
  - Establish credibility.

□ The Power of a Date

- ► Plus One or Plus None?
  - Friends: Your wingman/woman is always a great fit with no pressure.
  - Fulfilling friend: When you need that introduction you know your friend can make for you.
  - Co-worker: You can be fulfilling for each other.
  - No one at all: You can be your best date and a great exercise to build social confidence!

SHOWTIME

☐ The Power of Timing
- The early bird does get the worm!
- Call ahead if running late, you'll be excused!
- Make the event a priority!
- Plan transportation into your timing!
- Don't be the hang-er-on!

☐ The Power of Listening
- People love to talk about themselves...so let them!
- Gather information.
- Retain the conversation by taking notes at the event or on your way home.

☐ The Power of Conversation
- Is it cocktail talk, business talk, or your cocktail talking?
- Use your Power of Knowledge.
- Steer the conversation.
- Be a closer.
- Exiting a conversation.
- Conversation tactics the good and the bad:
  Loud talk – monitor your surroundings
  Over Talk – be polite
  Topic Tease – don't wear others out
  Babble Talk – put the drink down!
  "Me too" syndrome – don't fall into it
  Commonalities – make them known
  Breath – freshen it
  Space – give it
  Eye Contact – keep it
  Hand Gestures – make them
  Smile – do it
  Fidgeting – watch it!
  Cursing - don't $%#@ do it*
  Salaries and Ages – don't ask

Gossip – don't tell
Body Odor – cover it
Compliments – less is always more
Bad Jokes – don't make them
Knowing it all – you don't
Politics – respect and stay general

ENCORE, ENCORE!

☐ The Power of Follow Up and Follow Through
- ► The Two-Step
  - E-mail:
    - Send first thing the next morning!
  - Hand-written note:
    - Send a note or package in addition to an e-mail that can be easily deleted.
    - Include information or a product in your note that sends the message that you *listened* to them.
    - Special Delivery: Use a messenger, FedEx, UPS or USPS
    - Make a "date" by presenting opportunities and paying attention to events they may be at or want to attend.

- ► Build their Power Profile
  - Information Profile
  - Professional Profile
  - Academic Profile
  - Family Profile
  - Personal Profile
  - Event Profile
  - Relationship Profile
  - Communication Profile

☐ The Instant Replay
  ► Review and Improve.
    • What did and didn't work? How would you prepare differently? Add to your checklist for the next event or highlight steps you glossed over to make sure you become more productive at every event you attend!

SUCCEED!

HOW TO CONTACT LAURA SCHWARTZ

For more information on *Eat, Drink and Succeed*,
Laura Schwartz and her company,
White House Strategies, visit:

www.EatDrinkandSucceed.com

To schedule Laura for a speaking engagement,
media appearance or to inquire about bulk book order
opportunities for corporations, associations, nonprofits,
schools and universities, please contact:

Ashley Brooks, Vice President of Communications
312.643.1923 or Ashley@WhiteHouseStrategies.com

If you have a story of success using
The Networking Power of Social Events that you
would like to share with Laura, please e-mail:

Laura@EatDrinkandSucceed.com

NOTES